Weeder's Digest
The Best of GREENPRINTS

Edited by
PAT STONE

Fulcrum Publishing
Golden, Colorado

Library of Congress Cataloging-in-Publication Data

Weeder's digest : the best of GreenPrints / edited by Pat Stone.
        p.   cm.
    ISBN 1-55591-257-5 (pbk.)
    1. Gardening—Anecdotes. 2. Gardeners—Anecdotes. I. Stone,
Pat, 1949- . II. GreenPrints.
SB455.W43   1996
818' .54080836—DC20   96-26204
                                                            CIP

Printed in the United States of America

0 9 8 7 6 5 4 3 2 1

Fulcrum Publishing
350 Indiana Street, Suite 350
Golden, Colorado 80401-5093
(800) 992-2908 • (303) 277-1623

TABLE OF CONTENTS

ACKNOWLEDGMENTS

I'd like to gratefully acknowledge:

Renee Shepherd, the Patron Saint of GREENPRINTS;

Susan and Franklin Sides, the cofounders of GREENPRINTS, for all the hours and energy they contributed that first long year;

Don Wright and Ronnie Shushan, for voluntarily creating and donating the basic graphic design of the magazine;

Katrina Nicke and Peter Loewer, for all their personal encouragement and support;

Jeff Taylor, Diana Wells and all the other writers who've shared their wonderful words for little more than praise and pin money;

Sandra Brooks Mathers, Jean Jenkins, Marilynne Roach, Leila Cabib, Jack Vaughan, Elizabeth Allegretti, Dawn Jarvis, Andrew Sudkamp, Bianc Iano Davis, George Hendricks, Derek Collins and all the other artists whose illustrations have given life to type;

Kate Jaynes, Ray and Peg Prag, Will Rap, Nancy Phillips, Becky Baxter, Paulette Rickard, Thomas Powell, Dick Kennedy, Bill Novak and all the other advertisers who've supported the magazine;

Horticulture, Fine Gardening, American Gardener, National Gardening and the other garden magazines who've been kind enough to review GREENPRINTS and refer writers to it;

The thousands of subscribers who've had the guts to buy a

garden magazine that has no useful information at all;

Carol Clark and the gang at Fulcrum for having the guts to publish a book that shares the absolute best of said magazine;

You, for buying it (thanks!);

My family—Becky, Nate, Jesse, Sammy and Tucker—for all the many, many hours they've worked on mailings and other "fun jobs" for this magazine;

And God, who has blessed me in so many, many ways.

P.S. If you get the impression that GREENPRINTS owes its existence and health to the contributions and caring of many, many people, you are completely correct.

INTRODUCTION

Fellow Gardeners, prepare yourself for some of the most entertaining reading of your gardening life. Expect to chuckle and to cry. To be challenged and consoled. To be given new sight into an old activity. Ladies and Gentlemen, you are in for a wonderful time.

But first, let me tell you a story.

Late fall, 1989: I knew it was coming to an end. For twelve fine years, I'd been Garden Editor at *Mother Earth News* magazine. Now the handwriting was on the wall. It was only a matter of time before the new owner shut down our western North Carolina offices—and jobs—and moved the publication to (gulp) New York City.

What to do? I loved raising my family in these mountains; I deeply enjoyed editing and gardening. The obvious solution? Start my own magazine. But compete with the one hundred other how-to garden mags and newsletters already out there? Impossible! What to do?!

The question had preyed on my mind for weeks. Time was running out at dear ol' *Mother.*

Then one day I was driving home from work. I rounded the bend where valley, farmland and mountains suddenly open up to view, and just then, a little brainstorm tapped on my skull:

"How about a magazine that *doesn't* tell how to garden, but covers the personal, *human* side instead?"

That, in a beanpod, is how this book came to be.

It has been quite an adventure editing, proofing, selling, promoting, designing, financing, pasting, organizing, mailing, advertising, etc., a one-family publication. (Becky, my wife, handles circulation. The four kids—Nate, Jesse, Sammy and Tucker—chip in on fun-filled chores like renewal mailings.) One thing totally surprised me: how many different types of effort go into creating a home publishing business. I wouldn't call it overwhelming, but I'd certainly call it *whelming.*

But another thing didn't surprise me at all: the amount of remarkable writing GREENPRINTS has evoked and been able to share. I don't think any part of this venture gives me greater pleasure than discovering a new manuscript that just *rings* with focus and feeling. People *care* about gardening. Most of us do it out of love, out of a personal desire to get what plants already have: roots in the earth. So while practical information will always be the essential backbone of garden writing, there is a valued place for its opposite. GREENPRINTS's real achievement has been to tap the largely unexpressed *heart* of America's most popular outdoor activity. The joy. The frustration. The humor. The insights. The peace.

And you, oh best-beloved and fortunate reader, now have in your palms the chance to relish the essence of these efforts: the best forty pieces from GREENPRINTS's first five years. In the next 193 pages, you'll find words that sing with tenderness. Tales that chortle with the voice of experience: *bad* experience. (Maybe "humor" and "humble" have the same word root—namely *"humus"!*) Moments that shimmer with hard-won wisdom and heartfelt vision. Stories that dig deep into the frustrating, invigorating, evolving, perplexing and inspiring relationships we humans have with our plants.

I'm really tempted to take you by the hand and give you a guided tour: "'My Ninety Acres'—now, *there's* a classic! Say, don't skip by 'The Joy of NonGardening'—that Jeff Taylor *knows* funny! Oh, watch out for 'Weeds Are Us'; it definitely changed the way *I* think about gardening. And be sure—"

But it's better, I know, to herewith step back and let you discover the *Weeder's Digest* for yourself. And so I shall. Enjoy!

—*Pat Stone,* Editor

Spring

ON THE ART OF GARDENING

Spring bursts forth in joyous prose.
By Karel Čapek

❀　　❀　　❀

When I was only a remote and distracted onlooker of the accomplished work of gardens, I considered gardeners to be beings of a peculiarly poetic and gentle mind, who cultivate perfumes of flowers listening to the birds singing. Now, when I look at the affair more closely, I find that a real gardener is not a man who cultivates flowers; he is a man who cultivates

the soil. He is a creature who digs himself into the earth, and leaves the sight of what is on it to us gaping good-for-nothings. He lives buried in the ground. He builds his monument in a heap of compost. If he came into the Garden of Eden he would sniff excitedly and say: "Good Lord, what humus!" I think that he would forget to eat the fruit of the tree of knowledge of good and evil; he would rather look round to see how he could manage to take away from the Lord some barrow-loads of the paradisaic soil. Or he would discover that the tree of knowledge of good and evil has not round it a nice dishlike bed, and he would begin to

3

mess about with the soil, innocent of what is hanging over his head. "Where are you, Adam?" the Lord would say. "In a moment," the gardener would shout over his shoulder; "I am busy now." And he would go on making his little bed.

If a real gardener came into the Garden of Eden he would sniff excitedly and say: "Good Lord, what humus!"

If gardeners had been developing from the beginning of the world by natural selection they would have evolved most probably into some kind of invertebrate. After all, for what purpose has a gardener a back? Apparently only so that he can straighten it at times, and say: "My back does ache!" As for legs, they may be folded in different ways; one may sit on the heels, kneel on the knees, bring the legs somehow underneath, or finally put them round one's neck; fingers are good pegs for poking holes, palms break clods or divide the mould, while the head serves for holding a pipe; only the back remains an inflexible thing which the gardener tries in vain to bend. The gardener usually ends above in his seat; legs and arms are straddled, the head somewhere between the knees, like a grazing mare. He is not a man who would like "to add at least a cubit to his stature"; on the contrary, he folds his stature into half, he squats and shortens himself by all possible means; as you find him he is seldom over one metre high.

Tilling the soil consists, on the one hand, in various diggings, hoeings, turnings, buryings, loosenings, pattings, and smoothings, and on the other in ingredients. No pudding could be more complicated than the preparation of a garden soil; as far as I have found out, dung, manure, guano, leafmould, sods, humus, sand, straw, lime, baby's powder, saltpetre, horn, phosphates, droppings, cow dung, ashes, peat, compost, water, beer, knocked-out pipes, burnt matches, dead cats, and many other substances are added. All this is continually mixed, stirred in, and flavoured; as I said, the gardener is not a man who smells a rose, but who is persecuted by the idea that "the soil would like some lime," or that it is heavy (as lead the gardener says), and "would like some sand." Gardening becomes a scientific affair. A rose in

flower is, so to speak, only for dilettanti; the gardener's pleasure is deeper rooted, right in the womb of the soil. After his death the gardener does not become a butterfly, intoxicated by the perfumes of flowers, but a garden worm tasting all the dark, nitrogenous, and spicy delights of the soil.

Now in spring gardeners are irresistibly drawn to their gardens; as soon as they lay the spoon down, they are on the beds, presenting their rumps to the splendid azure sky; here they crumble a warm clod between their fingers, there they push nearer the roots a weathered and precious piece of last year's dung, there they pull out a weed, and here they pick up a little stone; now they work up the soil round the strawberries, and in a moment they bend to some young lettuce, nose close to the earth, fondly tickling a fragile tuft of roots. In this position they enjoy spring, while over their behinds the sun describes his glorious circuit, the clouds swim, and the birds of heaven mate. Already the cherry buds are opening, young foliage is expanding with sweet tenderness, blackbirds sing like mad; then the gardener straightens himself, eases his back, and says thoughtfully, "In autumn I shall manure it thoroughly, and I shall add some sand."

But there is one moment when the gardener rises and straightens himself up to his full height; this is in the afternoon, when he administers the sacrament of water to his little garden.

5

Then he stands, straight and almost noble, directing the jet of
water from the mouth of the
hydrant; the water rushes in a
silver and kissing shower; out of
the puffy soil wafts a perfumed
breath of moisture, every little
leaf is almost wildly green, and
sparkles with an appetizing joy,

so that a man might eat it. "So, and now it is enough," the
gardener whispers happily; he does not mean by "it" the little
cherry tree covered with buds, or the purple currant; he is thinking of the brown soil.

And after the sun has set he sighs with deep content: "I
have sweated today!"

Čapek, Karel. Illustrated by Josef Čapek. *The Gardener's Year.* (Madison: The University of
Wisconsin Press.) Reprinted by permission of the University of Wisconsin Press.

2

BILL, THE GARDEN CAT

Definitely uninvited. Most definitely disgusting.
Most completely definitely irreplaceable.

By Duane Campbell

✻　　✻　　✻

Bill walked in about eight years ago. He marched over to the food dishes, ate his fill, threw up, and fell asleep.

The last thing we needed was another pet. We already had a dog, two cats, a parrot, and miscellaneous smaller birds and beasts. But it's not as if we were asked.

The cat that moved into our house that day would have been thrown out of any respectable barn. Or alley, for that matter. Well past his prime (if he ever had a prime), he was nothing but skin and bones and appetite. His coat was appalling; mange comes to mind, but that is somehow inadequate. Chronic tooth problems gave him breath that could strip paint, and on those rare occasions when he washed himself, the stench permeated his whole body—indeed, the whole room, and the white patches of fur turned brown. He drooled unremittingly, and his hobby was, well, barfing.

Why *keep* such a cat? We really weren't consulted. The other animals, normally fiercely territorial, welcomed him instantly as part of the family. Besides, we quickly discovered a purr that could rattle the dishes in the cupboard along with a sense of … I'd guess you call it humanity. Strong as a lion, he was nonetheless gentle as a lamb: When he decided to leave

7

your lap, he left—no power could hold him—but there was never a scratch left behind.

Bill became my garden cat. As I stooped over a bed, I would prepare myself for the thump as he landed gracelessly on my back, where he would stretch out and languorously rest a damp chin on my shoulder, watching to make sure I did everything to his satisfaction. After I threw him off five or six times, he might grudgingly retreat to a ladder that hung horizontally on the side of the garage, where he would continue his observation, lanky legs stretched out fore and aft and belly spilling over the ladder rail. Unrestricted by my shoulder, the ever-present string of drool would elongate to several inches, swinging in the breeze, sometimes catching the sun in tiny rainbows. What a cat.

Supervision was his forte, but he was not above lending a paw where he saw the need. I never got seeds planted to suit him, for example, so he had to rearrange any newly planted bed. And he took a special interest in fertilization. All cats love the loose, freshly spaded soil of a seed bed, and commercial repellants won't even slow down a cat with a mission.

So for many years, my first assignment every morning was a walk through the garden, a cup of coffee in one hand, a small shovel with a very long handle in the other. Eventually I found a partial solution. Over the years I had accumulated small scraps of hardware cloth, chicken wire, and miscellaneous fencing—the sort of thing normal people would throw out. Tossing pieces on the soil surface where seeds were planted prevented the cats from scratching, and they lost interest. As soon as the seedlings showed, the bed seemed less enticing, and the cover came off.

Bill didn't resent these measures, just as I never resented his peculiar ministrations. Those of us who love living things, plant and animal alike, have learned what compromise really means.

Years after discovering this trick, I still make my morning walk. It has become a habit. And the truth is that I'm not a very methodical person, so the protective cover is sometimes forgotten, and the news quickly goes out to every cat in the neighborhood. But the real lesson is that, except for brief moments that are less than inspiring, it is a pleasant outing. I get to greet each plant on a daily basis, inquire of its health, and enjoy the garden for a while with a cup of coffee in my hand instead of a hoe.

For many years, Bill joined me every morning, strolling at my feet—drooling and belching, purring and coughing—but no longer.

Bill died this summer. He went softly, with the dignity that was so surprisingly a part of him. Oh, we've lost pets before, and we will again, and it always hurts. But this elderly stray was indefinably special. He slept with my daughter, watched TV with my wife, but he was my buddy, my garden cat, and I'll miss him.

That night we talked about the empty spot in our lives and decided there would be no rush to fill it. We had our Princess, an elegant dowager of sixteen-plus years, who no longer adapted well to changes in the family composition, and she deserved our concentrated attention in her remaining time. I would learn to work alone. Besides, how could a cat like Bill be replaced?

Five days after I had buried Bill under the lilac where he liked to sleep on hot afternoons, I was sitting crosslegged in the middle of the lawn contemplating thatch. From nowhere a tiny, orange-striped ball of fur and energy came racing. He jumped on my lap and started purring. Our inquiries provided not a hint of his provenance, but I think his orders came from under a lilac, issued by a spirit who knew I needed help in the garden. We named him Rufus, but after a couple of days his vitality earned him a soubriquet:

Illustration © Sandra Brooks Mathers

9

The Kitten from Hell. Nothing that moved was safe. We loved him instantly.

Rufus doesn't drool or belch or choke, and he isn't much of a garden cat, not yet. He's too young to take his responsibility seriously. But he's learning. I have no doubt that as his youthful exuberance abates, my garden will benefit greatly from his stewardship. He sleeps with my daughter and watches TV with my wife. And the beat goes on.

There are those who resent cats in their garden. As a newspaper columnist, the most frequent question I get is how to keep them out. But these people love their garden too much, and they miss a larger vision of love. If a genie appeared and offered me three wishes for the gardeners of the world, those wishes would be for a prosperous garden, a fine cat to share it with, and a good shovel with a very long handle.

3

VOLUNTEERS

Plants, and children, sometimes blossom in unexpectedly delightful ways.

By Clairborne Dawes

❋   ❋   ❋

The usual euphemism for them is "volunteers."

Not the neighbors' sons whom you dragoon into a morning of hauling out maple saplings, but plants, the ones that arrive unbidden in your favorite perennial bed or shrub border. Usually single, often tough, they are seldom tentative. They needed determination to get there, with no visible parents or even close relatives. Weeds arrive in numbers; these are—volunteers.

New England's soil is acid. Challenged also by the shade from tall white pines surrounding our yard, I often accept volunteers in my garden. The first, and perhaps my favorite, thrust roughly upward through a clump of blue campanulas one spring, shouldering aside their delicate stems as it grew, and grew, and grew. First offended, then curious, I let it have its way. In midsummer, my tolerance was rewarded with brilliant orange-yellow flowers, spreading in flat umbels atop the two-foot stalk: butterfly-weed, and the monarch butterflies hovered over it with delight. It threw off any design or color coordination I had planned, but I couldn't help enjoying my wayward, undisciplined volunteer.

That same summer, our daughter hit puberty. The verb correctly implies impact. Never docile, she still surprised us

with her sullenness, her explosions of thwarted rage. Her en-
thusiasms were equally violent, equally unexpected. My husband and I, unrebellious products of the unquestioning fif-
ties, learned to be alert for the warning tick of another bomb,
more fireworks.

As things got out of hand indoors, I found myself more
often in the garden. Here was order, even a semblance of control. Colors were blending, borders gently curving to reveal a
flowering shrub or two. With care, feeding, and much raking
of pine needles, a lawn was also emerging.

Then the hawkweed arrived: two or three vagrants at first,
on the edges of the lawn, easy to lop off with the lawnmower.
Soon, however, the flat crowns of leaves crept toward the sun-
nier places, dotting the grass with yellow and orange as summer advanced. They are with us still, spreading islands of
brightness. We try our best to avoid them with the mower.

The mullein came next. In a dull but serviceable patch of
pachysandra near the garage, it began as a small, furry rosette
of greyish leaves. Puzzled but not displeased, I left it alone.

Illustrations © Jean Jenkins

Suddenly, there was a stalk. Taller and
taller it became, more and more its
presence dominated that quarter of
the yard, yet it seemed a shame to pull
it up after all its effort. Besides, its
roots were tenacious.

About this time, a newcomer
showed up in our house. Our sunny,
carefree son was replaced by an in-
creasingly silent young man who
joined us, glum but ravenous, at meal-
times. In between, he kept to himself,
or his mates, and he grew, and grew.
Deprived of his company, baffled and dismayed by our
daughter's moods, I withdrew again to the garden.

The mullein had been busy. Atop that sturdy stalk clustered tightly closed buds which, one by one, opened to reveal
charming yellow florets. Incongruous in the pachysandra, it

nonetheless gave me great pleasure, and I pointed it out to my husband on our evening walk around the garden. He showed me another, not far away. It, too, would soon be blooming.

With high school's opening in September, our children turned their churning energies in new directions. Cal joined the band. Between Sousa marches, he and his clarinet made wild and gloomy music behind his closed door.

Betsy, for whom getting out of bed had seemed to cause muscle strain, was suddenly a cheerleader. Bare of leg, bouncy in her skimpy crimson skirt, she strutted and pranced, waving with delight when she saw us in the grandstand. Decades from Miss Euphemia's strict boarding school, where we young ladies had learned to turn up our noses at such plebeian goings-on, I gloried in her performance, her freedom, and her newly healthy psyche. Between games, I plied her with vitamin C against the knee-chilling November winds.

That summer, our daughter hit puberty. The verb correctly implies impact.

As winter approached, I fussed at the garden, mulching it, tucking it in. A barberry had appeared near the children's old sandbox that was rapidly filling with pine needles. How pretty those red leaves would look next fall if the bush were moved near the rosy Japanese maple by the driveway.

For Christmas, by request, we treated Cal to his first live rock concert, and off he went with a gang to the Worcester Centrum. It must have been quite a night. Coming down late for breakfast, he wore a mildly defiant expression and a new, gold stud in one ear. Temporarily aghast, I couldn't help smiling at this show of self-confidence. My husband lifted an eyebrow, but I shook my head at him.

That was a noisy winter, with Cal's favorite bands rocking his room and Betsy practicing cheers to recorded accompaniment in hers. I studied garden catalogs, and we survived. With spring, it became apparent we had more volunteers. A heretofore-unnoticed wild cherry bloomed in the backyard, and honeysuckle blossomed gratefully where we'd yanked out several maple saplings.

13

One afternoon, I found Cal stretched in a lawn chair by the honeysuckles, untroubled by the small bees happily humming there. Eyes closed, shirt unbuttoned to the May sun, he was tootling a low, meditative but not unhappy tune on his clarinet.

"I haven't heard that before," I said, sitting down in another chair.

"I made it up," he said dreamily, eyes still shut.

"I like it."

"Thanks."

I closed my own eyes and breathed in the honeysuckles' sweetness.

"It's nice out here. Our yard, I mean," said Cal after a few minutes.

"Yes, it's lovely today."

"I mean, you know, it's not all neat and stuff. You let things grow how they want to, kind of. Where they like it best."

I hesitated, plunged. "Actually, I would like to move just one, a barberry."

"Sure, Ma. Easy. Tomorrow." The tune began again.

I stripped off my gloves, let my trowel slip to the grass. No rush. Tomorrow would be fine.

4

The Best of Mornings

An early riser blessed by the incense of spring.

By Edwin F. Kalat

❂   ❂   ❂

I always rise very early in the morning. When you are an early riser, you cannot understand—to the point of irritation—any person who likes to sleep late. I have an alarm clock in my genes that tells me when it's 5:00 A.M., and that's when I have awakened all my life.

I've been hated and despised for this trait. I was practically lynched when my college dorm mates discovered who took a noisy shower every dawn. My new marriage almost ended in a quick divorce when my bride realized that I spring from sleep at 5:00 with a song on my lips. (She could sleep all day without difficulty.) Well, after 35 years and four children—which I fed during the night—she has grudgingly learned to accept this habit. But I must say I do not sing anymore.

I think it's a gross pity that millions of people go through life never experiencing a sunrise or the biological surge of a new day. If you've never seen or felt it, you will never know the joy that comes when the sound of birds singing mingles with the odor of freshly brewed coffee, or the delight of new sunlight splashing on a piece of toast.

In order to pray most properly, you must, like a monk, get up very early. An exuberant rendition of "Amazing Grace" might help, but actually there is no need for words—in the early morning, He's here. Oh, I know God is always around, but you just can't hear Him or feel His presence other times like you can at the break of day. Perhaps the birds sing just for that reason.

Every morning is wonderful, but for me, there are two or three days in May which are extraordinary. You see, I've been a gardener since I was a little boy. I guess to be a good farmer or gardener you almost have to be an early riser. Anyway, the experience I'm talking about most often occurs in May. You get up, strap on the old bib overalls, and find the old grizzled digging boots. You put on the tattered sweater that has the pockets mended with different color threads. Then you head outdoors.

It's cold. The sun has not risen, but there is light in the east. You start digging, making neat rows. The ground is dark and cold. It takes a while to warm to the exercise.

Suddenly, spontaneously, the sunlight explodes.

You could be awed by many mighty things on a morning such as this. You could be exhilarated by the music of the birds. You could be absorbed by the hues, aroma, and texture of flowers or bright gleam of the sunlight. Yes, yes, all of these.

And more. As the sun blends intimately with the soil, wisps of iridescent vapors curl, slowly at first, from the soil—like Abel's blessed smoke. More, more vapors form and rise until there is a cloud sparkled and rayed by the sun to an exotic brilliance.

At that moment you can only stand motionless in awe. The vapors exude the aroma of the earth, a perfume hearty and basic. The whole world feels green.

There is a noise or gust of wind and the moment is gone. But He was there.

So, too, was my prayer.

THE PANSY PEOPLE

A village of flowers that never met a stranger.

By Susan Strahan

✳   ✳   ✳

When I was a child, my mother used to take me to visit some friends of hers who lived in a neat little brick house on the other side of town. They had two children about my age. To be truthful, I scarcely remember them. I don't remember talking with them or playing with them, though I know I did both. What I remember are the pansies.

Illustrations © Jean Jenkins

There was a nice backyard with metal lawn chairs where the adults sat and talked. Near the chairs were two young trees—not yet big enough to give shade—circumscribed by a bed of pansies. I remember lying on the carpet of St. Augustine grass and whispering to them, watching them, and listening to them. There was a whole village of people under those trees. They were smiling, nodding, milling around, and gossiping. I remember these people with their round winking faces better than the children who would eventually drag me away to play.

Now the powers-that-be have invented pansies without faces. The woman at the nursery explained to me, quite matter-

17

of-factly, how "superior" these face-less flowers were. They produce five times more blooms than old-fashioned pansies. While I found the number impressive, I had to bite my tongue to keep from shouting into her face, "What good are more flowers if they haven't any faces?" I'd  hate to get up in the morning and see their slack one-eyed stares as I linger by the flower bed with a cup of hot cocoa.

I sort of pity them when they've been mixed in with all the "little people" pansies. In the village of old-fashioned pansies there are mustachioed men flirting with women with florid complexions, children with whiskers like a cat bobbing and weaving in the crowd, senoritas hiding shyly behind flamboyant fans, and owl-eyed professors who gravely nod their heads while apparently lecturing a pack of adolescents wearing too much make-up. And there's always the low murmur of conversation—or is that the hum of some low-flying bee? Alert-looking and approachable, these pansies have never met a stranger. It is almost impossible not to pause, exchange greetings, and strain to pick up some snatch of conversation. Mixed in with that crowd, the solid-colored pansies look like village idiots, every trace of intelligence and personality wiped from their faces.

As I pause in the nursery by the masses of blank-eyed pansies, all looking sort of stupidly cheery, with five times as many heads as the ones I'm buying, I can't help but think that someone out there is breeding a race of imbeciles—and pray that they don't take over the pansy world.

Still, I *can* walk by a bedful of these dim one-eyed horrors without shuddering. Without anything (like a real pansy) to remind me that these were once the men and women I conversed with in the flower bed, my mind simply lumps them together in that broad category of "flowers." Like the children I used to visit, their presence scarcely registers.

6

"MY NINETY ACRES"

A love story.

By Louis Bromfield

✦   ✦   ✦

I had a friend, a little old man, who lived over the hill in Possum Run Valley in a small white house on a farm which is known as "My Ninety Acres." It has never been given that name as farms are named "Long View" or "Shady Grove." The name is not painted on the red barn nor on a fancy sign hanging at the end of the lane leading up to the house; nevertheless throughout the Valley everybody always refers to Walter Oakes' farm as "My Ninety Acres." At first, years ago when Walter was still a young and vigorous man, they used to speak of "My Ninety Acres" with a half mocking, half affectionate smile, especially the big farmers who owned a lot of land, because Walter always talked about that ninety acres as if it were a ranch of many thousand acres like the vast King Ranch in Texas, or a whole empire. Some of the old farmers, I think, believed Walter a bumptious and pretentious young man.

But at last as time passed, and Walter turned into a solid middle-aged farmer and later into an old man, the smiles and mild sense of mockery went out and "My Ninety Acres" became simply the name of the place the way a farm was known as the Ferguson place or the Anson place. People said, "I'm going over to 'My Ninety Acres'" or "If you want to see a nice farm, go and have a look at 'My Ninety Acres.'" Old Walter had earned the right to say "My Ninety Acres" as Augustus Caesar might say "My Empire."

He had a right to speak of it with pride. It wasn't the conventional Currier and Ives farm one expects from the long tradition of American farming—a bright, new place, with new wire fences, and cattle standing like wooden animals in a pasture that was more like a lawn than a pasture. There was, indeed, a certain shagginess about it, a certain wild and beautiful look with that kind of ordered romantic beauty which was achieved by the landscape artists of the eighteenth century who fell under the influence of Jean Jacques Rousseau's romantic ideas regarding Nature.

The patches of lawn were kept neatly mowed, but surrounding them grew a jungle of old-fashioned flowers and shrubs—lilacs, standing honeysuckle, syringa, bleeding heart, iris, peonies, tiger lilies, day lilies, old-fashioned roses like the Seven Sisters and the piebald and the Baltimore Belle. At the back, the little vegetable garden was neat enough with its rows of vegetables and its peach and pear and quince trees in a row inside the white picket fence. But beyond the borders of the garden, the shagginess continued. There weren't any bright, new, clean wire fences. The wire along the fence rows was hidden beneath sassafras and elderberry and wild black raspberry and the wood lot on the hill above the creek was not a clean place with the grass eaten short by cattle. The cattle had been fenced out and the trees, from seedlings to great oaks, grew rankly with a tropical luxuriance.

But despite the shagginess of the farm's appearance, no fields in the Valley produced such big crops or pastured such fine cattle and hogs. At "My Ninety Acres" the shagginess didn't exist, the neighbors came to understand, because Walter was lazy or a bad farmer—there was no more hardworking man in the whole Valley. They were that way because Walter wanted them like that—Walter and Nellie.

I never saw Nellie Oakes. I am 48 years old and Nellie died before I was born when she gave birth to her second son,

Robert. But my father told me about her. In his time she had been the most beautiful girl in the Valley and she taught school at the Zion school house until, when she was 22, she married Walter Oakes. I think Nellie was beautiful rather than pretty because of her look of intelligence. Even today, you sometimes hear old people say, "Nellie Oakes was a mighty smart girl— the only woman I ever knew who was as smart as she was pretty."

People wondered why she chose him when she might have married Homer Drake, whose father owned 450 acres of the best land in the county, or Jim Neilson, whose family owned the bank and the feed mill in Darlington. She could have had her choice of any of the catches of the Valley and she chose Walter Oakes, who had no more than ninety acres of poor hill land he had just bought because he didn't have money enough for anything better.

My father was a gentle man. He never went through the Valley without stopping at "My Ninety Acres" and usually I was with him. Sometimes when we stopped at "My Ninety Acres" for a meal or for the night, I stayed and played about the barn with Robert Oakes, who was two years older than I, and his brother John, who was two years older than Robert. Sometimes if it was a Sunday we went fishing or swimming. Sometimes I simply trudged behind my father and Walter Oakes and his two sheep dogs as they walked about "My Ninety Acres," and as I grew a little older, I sometimes wondered that the two men could be together, walking side by side, perfectly happy, without talking at all. I did not know then what I came to know later, that among men who were as close as my father and Walter Oakes, conversation wasn't necessary. They knew without speaking what the other felt when a lazy possum, out in the middle of the day when he shouldn't have been, lumbered across the pasture and out of sight and scent of the dogs (I've seen Walter call the dogs and keep them by his side till the possum had disappeared, safe in some deep hole or hollow log).

And I was always a little surprised at how often Walter would say, "Nellie wanted me to put this field into pasture,

21

but we couldn't afford not to use it for row crops," or "It's funny how many good ideas a woman can have about farming. Now, Nellie always said … ." Sometimes in the warm summer heat, I'd return to the house, still trudging along behind the two grown men and the dogs, believing that I would find there the Nellie whom I had never seen, who was dead before I was born, waiting for us with a good supper on the table.

"Nellie Oakes was a mighty smart girl—the only woman I ever knew who was as smart as she was pretty."

People in the Valley couldn't see why Walter Oakes didn't get married again. They said, "He's still a young man and he's done a wonderful job with 'My Ninety Acres,'" or "I don't see how a man like that can get on without a woman at his age. It ain't natural." And a good many widows and spinsters past their first youth certainly set their caps for him. It wasn't only that he was doing well with "My Ninety Acres." He was, as I remember him then, a big, straight, clean, good-looking fellow with his sun-tanned face, blue eyes, and blond hair bleached by the sun. He would, I think, have pleased even a young girl.

But Walter never showed any signs of marrying again. He was always polite and his eyes sometimes twinkled with humor when he saw what some of the good ladies were up to.

The two boys were nice kids and smart like Nellie. John, the older one, looked like her, with dark eyes and dark hair. Robert, the younger one, who had never seen his mother, looked like Walter. The father wanted both of them to go to college and get a good education. I think Walter always loved John, the older one, best—not because of any resentment of Robert because he had caused his mother's death but because John looked so much like Nellie.

With all my family, I went away from the county when I was 17 and I was gone for 25 years. Sometimes at first my father heard from Walter, rather brief, unsatisfactory and inarticulate letters, written on lined paper torn out of a copybook, but neither Walter nor my father were very good letter writers.

They were both the kind of men who could not communicate without the warmth that came of physical presence. Writing letters didn't mean much. When they met again, even after years, the relationship would be exactly the same. They were that kind of men, and that kind of friends.

I know very little of the details of what happened during those years. The war came and in it, John, the older son, whom Walter secretly loved best, was killed at St. Mihiel. He was 21 and just finished with agricultural college. Walter had counted on his returning to the farm, marrying, and producing grandchildren to carry it on. Robert, when he returned from the war, did not stay on the farm. He was very smart, like Nellie, but he didn't want to be a farmer.

Robert had ambitions. He had had them even as a small boy. Sometimes when the three of us, as kids, sat naked among the wild mint by the swimming hole, we talked about what we were going to do in life and Robert always said, "I'm going to be a great man and get rich and have an automobile with a man to drive it."

In the 25 years I was away from the Valley, Robert had achieved exactly what he had planned. By the time I returned, Robert was president of the Consolidated Metals Corporation and he had made many millions of dollars. I think he must have had both Nellie's "smartness" and Walter's steadfastness.

In the first weeks after I came home, I never thought about my father's friend, old Walter Oakes. And then one day I heard Wayne, one of the boys on the farm, say something about "My Ninety Acres" and I remembered it all and asked, "Is Walter Oakes still alive?"

"Alive!" said Wayne, "I'll say he's alive. The livest old man in the county. You ought to see that place. Brother, that's the kind of farm I'd like to own. He raises as much on it as most fellows raise on five times that much land."

The next Sunday I walked over the hills to "My Ninety Acres." As I came down the long hill above the farm, I saw that it hadn't changed much. The house still looked well-painted and neat with its white walls and green shutters, and the barn was a bright new

Illustrations © Derek Collins

prosperous red. But the shrubs and flowers had grown so high that they almost hid the house. It was a day in June, and as I walked down the long hill, the herd of fat, white-faced cattle stood knee-deep in alfalfa watching me.

The corn stood waist-high and vigorous and green, the oats thick and strong, the wheat already turning a golden yellow. In the meadow, the bumblebees were working on clover that rose almost as high as a man's thighs. In all that plenty there was something almost extravagant and voluptuous. The rich fields were like one of the opulent women painted by Rubens, like a woman well-loved whose beauty thrives and increases by love-making.

By now, of course, I remembered enough to know that I should find old Walter somewhere in the fields. Sunday afternoon he always spent walking over the place.

So I went down toward the creek and as I turned the corner by the barnyard, I saw him down below moving along a

fence row. Two sheep dogs were with him, the great-great-great grandchildren of the pair I had known as a boy. They were running in and out of the hedgerow yapping joyously. I stood for a moment, watching the scene. There was something lonely about the figure of the old man wandering along the fence row filled with sassafras and elderberry. For no reason I could understand, I felt a lump come into my throat.

Then I noticed that there was something erratic in the progress of the old man. He would walk a little way and then stop and, parting the bushes, peer into the tangled fence row. Once he got down on his knees and for a long time disappeared completely in the dark clover.

Finally, as he started back along the far side of the field, I set off down the slope toward him. It was the barking of the dogs as they came toward me that attracted his attention. He stopped and peered in my direction, shading his eyes with his big hands. He was still tall and strong, although he must have been over seventy, and only a little stooped. He stood thus until I was quite near him, and then I saw a twinkle come into the bright blue eyes.

"I know," he said, holding out his hand. "You're Charley Bromfield's boy. I heard you'd come back."

I said I'd been trying to get over to see him and then he asked, "And your father. How's he?"

I told him my father was dead. "I'm sorry," he said, very casually as if the fact of death were nothing. "I hadn't heard. I don't get around much." I explained that my father had been ill for a long time and that death had come as a release.

Then suddenly he seemed to realize that I must have seen him for a long time, ducking and dodging in and out of the fence row. A faint tinge of color came into his face and he said shyly, "I was just snoopin' around my ninety acres. I like to see what goes on here and I don't get time during the week."

He looked down at his big hands and noticed, as I did, that some of the black damp loam of the fence row still clung to them. He brushed them awkwardly together. Then he said, "Come with me and I'll show you something."

I followed him along the fence row and presently he knelt and parted the bushes and beckoned to me. I knelt beside him and he pointed. "Look!" he said, and his voice grew suddenly warm, "Look at the little devils."

I looked and could see nothing at all but dried brown leaves

with a few delicate fern fronds thrusting through them. Old Walter chuckled and said, "Can't see 'em, can you? Look, over there by that hole in the stump." I looked and then slowly I saw what he was pointing at. They sat in a little circle in a tiny nest, none of them much bigger than the end of one of old Walter's big thumbs— seven tiny quail. They sat very still not moving a feather, lost among the dry, brown leaves. I might not have seen them at all but for the brightness of their little eyes.

"Smart!" he said, with the same note of tenderness in his voice. "They know! They don't move!"

Then a cry of "Bob White!" came from the thick, fragrant clover behind us and Walter said, "The old man's somewhere around." The whistle was repeated, again and then again.

Old Walter stood up and said, "They used to laugh at me for letting the bushes grow up in my fence rows, but they don't any more. When the chinch bugs come along all ready to eat up my corn, these little fellows will take care of 'em." He chuckled, "There's nothing a quail likes as much as a chinch bug. Last year Henry Talbot, down the road, lost 10 acres of corn all taken by the bugs. Henry's a nut for clear fence rows. He doesn't leave enough cover along 'em for a grasshopper. He thinks that's good farming, the old fool!" The old man chuckled again.

We were walking now up the slope from the creek toward the house, and he went on talking. "That fence row beside you is just full of birds—quail and song sparrows and thrushes—the farmer's best protection. It was Nellie that had that idea about lettin' fence rows grow up. I didn't believe her at first. I was just as dumb as most other farmers. But I always found out that Nellie was pretty right about farming. She was hardly ever wrong ... I guess never."

I said, "What became of Mrs. Ince, the housekeeper you hired?"

He said, "Oh, she got old and sick and went back to live with her sister. I just didn't get anybody to take her place."

"You mean you're living here all alone?" I asked.

"Yes."

I started to say something and then held my tongue, but old Walter divined what it was I meant to ask and said, "No. It ain't lonely. It doesn't seem to me like a farm is a lonely place. There's too much goin' on. Nellie used to say she didn't understand the talk of these women who said they got lonely. Nellie said there was always calves and horses and dogs and

27

lambs and pigs and that their company was about as good as most of them women who talked that way. And she always had her posy garden. Did you notice it coming in? It's mighty pretty right now. Nellie planted everything in it … just the way they are today." He was about to say something else, but checked himself and looked at me strangely. A secretive, almost sly look came into his eyes, and he turned away to stare at the glass he held in his hand.

After an awkward pause, I said, "Well, Robert did all right by himself. He always said he wanted a big automobile and a driver and a lot of money and he got it all right."

Then old Walter looked up at me and grinned, "Yes, I guess he got just about what he wanted. He's a good boy, but he's got some funny ideas." The old man chuckled. "He's been trying for years to get me to retire and live in the city where I could take it easy or go down and live in Florida. What'd I do with these big ugly hands in a place like that? I wouldn't know what to do with myself. And what would become of 'My Ninety Acres'?"

It was getting late and I rose, but the old man went on talking. "It's a pity about Robert not having any children. I guess his wife is all right. I don't see much of her. We don't have much in common. But it's a pity Robert couldn't have found a woman he could have loved."

That was the first and last time I ever heard him speak of his daughter-in-law, but out of the meager speech and the look in his eyes and the sound of his voice, I divined what she must be like. Indeed, I gained a very clear picture of her.

"Robert comes to see me about once a year and stays for a day or two, but he's a pretty busy man with all the big affairs he has to manage."

"Tell him to drive over and see me the next time he comes," I said. "And you come over, too."

He opened the screen door for me. "I'm afraid I don't get off 'My Ninety Acres' very often any more. You'll understand if I don't get over soon. The place takes a lot of time when you're working it alone."

I left him and the dogs at the gate and set out over the hill across the pasture with the fat, white-faced cattle, for home.

It wasn't the last time I saw old Walter. There was enough of my father in me to make the friendship between myself and the old man before very long nearly as warm as their friendship had been. And after all, between them, they had taught me many of the things I had come with experience to value most in life. The Sunday afternoon visits to "My Ninety Acres" became very nearly a habit, for I found gradually that old Walter was in himself an education. He knew more of the fundamentals of soil, of crops, of livestock than any man I have ever known. Some of them he had read in books and in farm papers, but he didn't trust the things he read until he tried them out, and many of them he didn't even attempt to try out since out of his own wisdom he understood at once that they were rubbish. Instinctively and out of experience, he rejected things which ran counter to the laws of Nature.

"Nellie," he would say, "always said that Nature and the land itself was the best answer to all these questions. If it wasn't natural it wasn't right, Nellie would say, and I've never found that she was wrong. She used to say that there were two kinds of farms—the 'live' farms and the 'dead' ones and you could tell the difference by looking at them. A 'live' farm was the most beautiful place in the world and a 'dead' farm was the saddest. It depended on the man who worked them—whether he loved the place and saw what was going on or whether he just went on pushing implements through the ground to make money."

One afternoon I arrived to find old Walter in the garden, standing quite still, staring at something. He did not speak when I came near him but only raised his hand in a gesture which clearly prohibited any speech or violent movement. Then he pointed at a male cardinal, very handsome in his red coat, moving restlessly about the lower branches of a magnolia and chirping anxiously. In a low voice he said, "The poor fellow is looking for his mate. I found her dead yesterday on the ground under that pine over there. He was staying around, trying to bring her back to life and make her fly away with him. I took her and buried her. I hoped he'd forget and fly away and find another mate. But he didn't. He keeps hanging around, trying to find her. It's funny about birds and animals that way."

And then one brilliant day in October, I saw a big, shiny black car coming up the long lane to our house. I knew at once who was in it. I knew by the size and importance of the car, and as it drew nearer, by the cut of the driver's uniform. It was Robert. He had come on his annual visit and had driven over to see me.

I went down the path to meet him and as he stepped out of the shiny car, it was hard for me to remember him as the boy I had seen the last time when he was 16, slim, muscular, towheaded, and athletic. He still looked a little like old Walter, yet in a strange way he appeared older than the old man. He was plump and rather flabby with pouches beneath the eyes which looked through the shining lenses of steel-rimmed spectacles. He stooped a little and there was a certain softness about his chin and throat.

He said, "I'm Robert Oakes. My father told me you had come back to live in the Valley."

"Yes, I know. I'm delighted to see you. Come in."

I found him rather as I had expected him to be, an intelligent fellow, with a good deal of dignity and authority. He was, after all, the child of old Walter and Nellie and their qualities could not be altogether lost in him. After 30 years the going was a little stiff at first, but after a drink we got together again, mostly by talking about "My Ninety Acres" and the old swimming hole in the creek and maple-sugar-making time and the other boyhood experiences we had shared.

I asked him to stay for lunch and he accepted the invitation so readily that I suspected he had counted on it from the beginning. I said, "I know it's no good sending for your father. He won't leave the place."

"No, he and Jed were in the field by the creek husking corn when I left." Robert laughed. "He told me if I sat around long enough over here I'd get a drink and be asked to lunch. He said it was worth it to see the house and the place. Privately, I think he wanted to get rid of me for most of the day so he could get on with his work. He doesn't know what to do with me. I get in his way and take up his time."

After lunch we sat for a time on the porch overlooking the Valley. And presently he came round to what was clearly the object of his visit. "I really wanted to talk about my father," he said. "He's quite a problem and stubborn as a mule. I know your father was a great friend of his and that he accepts you nowadays exactly as if you were your father. And I thought

31

you might have some influence with him. You see, I offered him almost everything—I've offered him a fruit ranch in Florida or Southern California, or a bigger farm, or a flat in New York. I've tried everything and he doesn't want any of it. He won't even let me hire him a couple or buy him an automobile or any machinery that might make life easier for him. This morning he was up at daylight and down husking corn in the bottom field with Jed by seven o'clock."

I grinned for I could see the whole picture and could understand how the old man's rich, famous, successful son got in his way.

"When I got up," said Robert, "I found some eggs and pancake batter laid out for me and coffee on the stove, with a note to my driver about how to get breakfast for me. In the note he said to come down to the bottom when I'd finished breakfast. What can you do with a fellow like that?"

"What do you want me to do?"

"I want you to persuade him to let me do something for him. He's 75 years old and I'm afraid something will happen to him alone there in the house or barn."

"I'm afraid it's no good," I said. "I couldn't persuade him any more than you."

"I've tried everything, even to saying, 'What would it look like if it came out in the papers that my father had died suddenly alone on his farm in Ohio?' That's pretty cheap, but even that didn't move him. All he said was, 'You're rich enough to keep it out of the papers and anyway the dogs would let people know if I was sick.'"

We were both silent for a time and then I said, "Honestly, Bob, I don't think there's anything to be done and to tell the truth I don't see why we should do anything. He's as happy as it's possible for a man to be. He's tough as nails and he loves that place like a woman." Then hesitantly, I said, "Besides, Nellie is always there looking after him."

A startled look came into the son's blue eyes and after a moment he asked, "Do you feel that way, too?" Nellie must have been as unknown and strange to Robert as she was to me.

I said, "I think Nellie is everywhere in that ninety acres. He's never lonely. She's in the garden and the fields and his famous fence rows. She's out there husking corn with him now in the bottom forty."

Robert lighted another cigar. "It's the damnedest thing," he said. "Sometimes I've felt that he had some resentment because I killed my mother when I was born or that he liked John better because he looked like her, but I know that isn't true. That's not in the old gentleman's character. I think it's more because Nellie is always there and I just get in his way. Sometimes," he added, "I think the old gentleman gets Nellie and the ninety acres a little mixed up."

We talked some more and then Robert called his driver, got in the shiny car, and drove off. We had agreed that there wasn't anything to be done about old Walter and Nellie. I said I'd keep my eye on him and go over myself or send somebody once every day to see that he was all right. Of course on Thursdays it wasn't necessary because that was the day that Jed's wife came to do the washing and clean up. And so every day for two years, I, or somebody from the place, went over. Sometimes we'd have an excuse but more often we didn't even let him know that he was being watched. One of us would drive past at chore time, or I'd walk over the hills and watch until he appeared in the barnyard or the garden. I knew how much he'd resent it if he suspected that anyone was spying on him, and I didn't want to risk breaking our friendship.

I continued to go over every Sunday, and each time I went over I learned something about soil or crops or animals, for the knowledge and experience of the old man seemed inexhaustible. And then one Sunday afternoon in early September when we were walking alone through one of old Walter's cornfields, I made a discovery. It was fine corn, the whole field, the best in the whole county, and as we came near the end of a long row, he stopped before a mighty single stalk of corn which was beautiful in the special way that only corn can be beautiful. It was dark green and vigorous and from it hung two huge nearly ripened ears and a third smaller one. Old Walter stopped and regarded it with a glowing look in his blue eyes.

"Look at that," he said. "Ain't it beautiful? That's your hybrid stuff." His hands ran over the stalk, the leaves and the ears. "I wish Nellie could have seen this hybrid corn. She wouldn't have believed it."

As I watched the big work-worn hand caressing that stalk of corn, I understood suddenly the whole story of Walter and Nellie and the ninety acres. Walter was old now, but he was vigorous and the rough hand that caressed that corn was the hand of a passionate lover. It was a hand that had caressed the body of a woman who had been loved as few women have ever been loved, so passionately and deeply and tenderly that there would never be another woman who could take her place. I felt again a sudden lump in my throat, for I knew that I had understood suddenly, forty years after the woman was dead, one of the most tragic but beautiful of all love stories. I knew now what Robert's strange remark about Nellie and the ninety acres getting mixed up had meant. Robert himself must once have seen something very like what I had just seen.

> *As I watched the big work-worn hand caressing that stalk of corn, I understood suddenly the whole story of Walter and Nellie and the ninety acres.*

It happened at last. I went over one Sunday afternoon a few weeks later and when I could not find old Walter or the dogs anywhere I returned to the house and went inside. I called his name but no one answered, and in a little while I heard scratching and whining in the ground floor bedroom and then a short bark and when I opened the door, the sheep dog bitch came toward me. The other dog lay on the hooked rug beside the bed, his head between his paws, looking at me mournfully as if he knew that I understood. On the bed lay old Walter. He had died quietly while he was asleep.

I telegraphed to Robert and he came with his wife for the funeral. The wife was exactly as I expected her to be and I understood what old Walter had meant when he said it was a pity Robert had never found a woman he could love. As I listened to the service, I knew how much feeling lay behind old Walter's simple observation.

He was buried beside Nellie in the Valley churchyard. The dogs came over to join my dogs and after a while they got on together. Robert wouldn't sell "My Ninety Acres," but I undertook to farm it for him and one of our men went there to live. But it will never be farmed as old Walter farmed it. There isn't anybody who will ever farm that earth again as if it were the only woman he ever loved.

7

Planting Out

*Sometimes the hardest part of gardening
is deciding—or remembering—what you're doing.*

By Geoffrey Charlesworth

✢ ✢ ✢

I am standing in the garden, a plant in my hand, in a state of indecision. Where shall I plant it?

I have a new raised bed ready for planting. I have just read an article in an Illinois newspaper where Waid Vanderpoel casually throws out that he has many large troughs each devoted to plants from a single geographic region. The Japanese trough, the Western trough, and so on. What elegance! I have decided to reserve my new bed for European plants. I think my plant is from the Caucasus, or is it Armenia? Is the Caucasus part of Europe, or Asia, or would it count as Asia Minor? Shall I go indoors and check the atlas before I plant it? Shall I make sure it really is from the Caucasus by looking it up in *Hortus* or the *RHS Dictionary*? It would mean tracking a bit of garden into the livingroom, and it would certainly mean washing my hands. How important is this geographical segregation? Suppose a plant has a wide range that includes a bit of Asia and a piece of Europe too, does it have a choice of troughs? Or are we talking about endemics? Perhaps I had better forget about geography and think about the plant.

It is a campanula. I think it is a low one. But what if it is like *C. alliariifolia* or *C. persicifolia*. It would look ridiculous in a raised bed with tiny alpines. I eye the perennial border. But suppose, after all, it is low; then I can't really put it with the peonies and the daylilies. Shall I go back to the library and look it up? I look at the name again. *C. betulaefolia.* Suddenly I remember; it is low and rather choice. I move towards a scree bed. Do campanulas really like scree? This bed is likely to get really hot sun in the summer; don't all campanulas like a bit of shade? Maybe on the east side of the raised bed falling in an ethereal blue waterfall down the cool side of the bed. I chuckle at my inspiration. No: if I plant it there it will surely grow towards the sun and therefore into the bed, and I wouldn't get the waterfall at all. How about a compromise: on the south side but near something large enough to give it a bit of shade? Oh, well, there isn't too much room there; I'd bet- ter find a place with more elbow room— after all, most campanulas like to run around a bit. I cross to another raised bed with a large maple giving afternoon shade. Now what else is in flower at the same time as campanulas? Maybe a dian- thus would be a good companion. Look, there is a place next to *Dianthus alpinus* 'Joan's Blood.' But would that color rather obliterate the campanula? And what about next year? *D. alpinus* is notoriously short-lived, and so there might not be a color combination at all. In any case I see that this *Alyssum saxatile* will need all the space up to the dianthus before long, and it won't leave much room for my campanula.

Finally I find a place that looks about right. I look at the neighbors. Bother, one of them is another campanula. *C.*

turbinata! It will never do to have two campanulas next to each other. First, they will encroach, and second, there will not be enough contrast. Third—and this clinches it—if one of the labels gets broken I won't know which plant belongs to the remaining label. Better to have one unknown campanula than two campanulas with one label. It is now 11:30, and the sun is getting high, if I don't find a spot quickly it may soon be too hot to plant out, and anyway lunch break is imminent. I wander over to a new bed. No: never put new seedlings into new soil; they invariably winter heave.

I go over to a favorite old bed and find a good general area. I look over the possibilities for a particular spot. I crouch to pull out a Johnny-jump-up, and there's another, and here's a dandelion, for goodness sake. I just did this bed. These weeds grow overnight. Soon I am engrossed in pulling weeds and realize I need my favorite cultivator and a weeder. I return to the barn and get the tools. My hands are soon full of weeds, and I need a bucket to put them in. I go back to the barn to get a bucket and thoughtfully bring back a large can of water ready for the final planting in. I plunge into this weedy area, and before long I am weeding a path while the campanula sits on the garden waiting patiently. On my left is a real mess of dead leaves that need clipping. I go back to the barn, now trudging a little, to get the clippers and return to clip off the old leaves. Underneath the soggy mess I find a saxifrage kicked out by the deer. Enraged, I pick it up and look for place to replant it. It falls apart in my hands. My feelings are now a weird mixture of grief and greed: I can't replant it, but I can pot it up into at least ten pieces. It will be great to have extra plants for the next plant sale. I put down my tools and return to the greenhouse, holding the saxifrage in both hands and moving, arms outstretched, with almost a slight waddle. I pot up some of the pieces and quickly run out of pots. I look around the greenhouse in vain and find I must go back to the barn and search for more. By now it's lunchtime, and after a quick bowl of soup I get back to potting saxifrage pieces. I water the divisions well, load the pots into a tray, and carry them to a cold frame. All the cold frames are full. These cuttings must have some protection for four or five days at least. I shall have to make room in the cold frame no matter what. I decide to remove a tray of plants and plant them out in the garden; this will give me the necessary space. I take the heavy tray and, now at full waddle, return down the garden looking for places to plant out my twenty plants. On the way I pass a campanula sitting on the garden.

Now what on earth is *that* doing there? How could anybody be so stupid as to leave a little campanula seedling standing in the middle of the garden? Look! It's *Campanula betulaefolia;* one of the best! I must get it in right away. Now where shall I put it?

From *The Opinionated Gardener* by Geoffrey Charlesworth. Copyright © 1987 by Geoffrey Charlesworth. Reprinted by permission of David R. Godine, Publisher.

8

Gladys's Tree

The cherished legacy of a defiant wife.

By Audrey Y. Scharmen

✣   ✣   ✣

"That tree whose leaves are trembling is yearning for something. ..."

A stanza, written nearly 600 years ago by a Castilian folk poet, wanders restlessly through my head as I kneel beneath the aged crab apple tree in my yard. It is time to plant this wild blue phlox I hold in my hand, but the air is chill and the damp black soil like that of the tomb. A stubborn spring refuses to make a commitment.

Pale violets peer hesitantly through the greening grass and ice-blue stars of periwinkle snuggle in satin leaves under the gnarled boughs. Brave blossoms of grape hyacinths and daffodils huddle together near the mossy trunk. But the apple tree's flowers are late—its rosy buds are tightly closed and it sighs, in a harsh blast of north wind from the creek, as I whisper words of encouragement.

Last autumn, the tree suffered a blow from a neighboring oak during a fierce nor'easter. Now it lists, slightly bent as though bearing an invisible burden, and I wonder how many more springtimes it will grace.

We have known one another for 15 years—this tree and I. Ours is a kind of mutual nurturing: I groan as I go about my

Illustrations © P. Savage

stooping and standing and squatting—the painful motions of
a gardener—and it responds in the soft murmuring way of
very old trees. But on this cruel day, I am dispirited and the
tree echoes my mood. Winter had been too long and dreary;
April—the coldest on record.

Impatiently I abandon my tools and the phlox and settle
in a sagging rocker in a sheltered corner of the porch to watch
the tree: A dozen waxwings have come to sup on the apple
blossoms—their biological clock tells them it is time—but there
are none. They gather on a budding branch and talk it over,
then rise in a flurry of golden feathers and suddenly are gone.

This tree, elderly and neglected, came into my life on an
April day when dogwood and redbud bloomed in unison and
the woodlands were tinged with many shades of green. My
partner and I were househunting Tidewater country, following daffodils down narrow rutted roads to dead-end coves
where weathered pilings tottered amid workboats heaped high
with rusting crabpots. Along the weedy shoreline, ancient trees
lined up to admire their reflections in the still water.

We had fled the city in search of a cozy place near the
water, perhaps an aged farmhouse with a cache of memories

and a friendly ghost or two. But many such houses already had been razed to make way for towering new condos of cedar and glass—with not a friendly facade in the entire lot.

It was the rosy glow of a pink cloud that finally beckoned us around a bend to the barren lot where stood a shabby cottage—vintage 1950's. Empty windows winked at us. A yellowed for-sale sign stuck to one of the panes. And in the corner of the yard stood the most beautiful crab apple tree in the county.

We parked and wandered into its dappled shade, to stare up at a maze of blossoming boughs where a redbird declared his love for the world and everything in it. Beyond lay a pale blue creek where workboats drowsed at the dock and heron stalked the shallows. The sweet sad cry of ospreys drifted above.

I groan as I go about my stooping and standing and squatting—the painful motions of a gardener—and it responds in the soft murmuring way of very old trees.

We were smitten. No matter the house didn't fit our dream. We would "fix" it. No matter that I, an aged wood nymph, had wanted our own forest. Thick woods were all around—I would share at a distance their autumn colors and hootings of owls and summer calls of whippoorwills. Such flaws were of no consequence—they were eclipsed by the dazzling charm of a single tree.

So we bought the fantasy—and it became a reality.

The tree is our calendar, a reflection of each season. In spring come transient waxwings to nibble at the sweet blossoms—and they return in autumn to glean the golden-fairy apples and to fill the yellow leaves with lisping whispers. Warblers and goldfinches graze the dense foliage of summer; and in late winter when the boughs are sometimes dusted with snow, migrant evening grosbeaks stop by to dine on the frosted fruit. Amid these winged Gypsies, a mockingbird with squatter's rights loudly complains as he attempts to protect his claim.

When the shrill cries of peepers rise from the warming creek to herald the vernal equinox, the first tiny nosegays of buds appear on the tree and we hover anxiously about the boughs until, in the pale sunlight of mid-April, the pink petals shyly unfurl to blend with darker buds in a variegated froth—a kind of delicious parfait of flowers. Heavy rains may fall—perhaps even some snow, but the newborn flowers cling tenaciously until a lingering warm spell coaxes them into maturity. There they languish while the days move lazily toward May and a thousand bees set the tree to murmuring contentedly.

Too soon the flowers grow pale and blowzy and fall in gentle showers. They raft-up on the creek and gather in pink wind-rows on the lawn. They drift aimlessly about as if reluctant to leave. Then, with a docile wind, they scurry along the lane, drowning the neighboring flowers in a wake of wilting apple blossoms.

Amazingly, this once was an unwanted tree, planted by the woman named Gladys—the lonely and childless wife of the man who built the cottage. He, dour and re-clusive, stripped this site of all the virgin timber, wild dogwood, and pink laurel that once framed the splendid view of the creek. The neighbors were dismayed, and the man's wife was very angry. With unaccustomed defiance, she planted a sapling in the corner of the empty yard beside the lane.

She cherished the tree, and it flourished and brought forth many blossoms in that very first spring as if to compensate for the senseless slaughter of all the others. The eccentric man merely tolerated it and declared there would be nothing else of the sort allowed in his yard.

The petite pink flowers of the simple tree far outshone even those of the dogwoods along the lane, and the neighbors took quite a fancy to them. Thus the apple tree became a kind of landmark—a symbol of springtime—known as "Gladys's Tree."

When the old man died several years later, Gladys soon followed. In autumn, the property was offered for sale. But throughout the long bleak winter it was ignored, until spring brought us together.

Since that day there have come summers of drought and winters of great snows, many capricious Aprils to test the endurance of an aged tree—and a hurricane of progress that has altered us all. The watermen's crab shacks are gone, bulkheads replace the marsh grass where the herons hunted, and little is left of the vast woodlands. Gone are the owls and the whippoorwills. Thus, the old apple tree is all the more cherished as a constant in our diminished world.

No tree is immortal, I muse, as I kneel again in the cold bed of the periwinkles. No amount of cherishing can alter destiny. But I see continuity in the pink buds of its very first offspring in a vacant lot across the lane.

I always think of Gladys as I dig amongst the wandering roots of her tree. I think of the rocker she left on the porch and how it sometimes moves gently to and fro on a windless night when the full-pink-moon of April fills the blossoming boughs with a ghostly glow and the mockingbird sings a rondo of nightingale notes. I think of the plaintive whispers heard in the cavelike coolness of the drooping branches when the cicadas sing their death songs on a melting August afternoon. Now I include, also, thoughts of a poet recording his laments in a time far more uncertain than this—yet harboring hope all the while.

Overhead a feeble ray of sunlight tumbles through the tangled limbs to reveal one full pink apple blossom amid the rosy buds of a bough, and in my heart I joyously sing one of the final lines of the Castilian's poem:

"They are already showing: come out and look!"

Stanza
By Diego Hurtado de Mendoza
(1364–1404)

That tree whose leaves are trembling
is yearning for something.

That tree so lovely to look at
acts as if it wants to give flowers:
it is yearning for something.

That tree so lovely to see
acts as if it wants to flower:
it is yearning for something.

It acts as if it wants to give flowers:
they are already showing; come out and look:
it is yearning for something.

It acts as if it wants to flower:
they are already showing; come out and see:
it is yearning for something.

They are already showing: come out and look.
Let the ladies come and pick the fruits:
it is yearning for something.

9

FERGUSON IN THE GARDEN

The dog with vinaigrette on his breath.

By Ellie MacDougall

*   *   *

For the past 11 years, I've had a constant companion in the garden. He's about two feet tall with short black fur and distinctly omnivorous tendencies. His name is Ferguson and he is my husband's Labrador Retriever.

At the age of four months, Ferguson discovered that hanging around the garden was not only a chance for an extra scratch behind the ears and a nap in the sun but also an opportunity to cadge some good eats. We lived in an apartment then and kept him on a 20-foot-chain during the day, away from the busy driveway. The tether was designed to hold sheep and goats so I thought it would be more than adequate for a baby Lab. Not so. When his curiosity about my poking around in the garden finally overcame him, he nonchalantly pulled the stake out of the ground and ambled over to poke his nose in the dirt, wagging his tail and dragging his chain behind him. He's been with me in the garden ever since.

We soon discovered that, along with the typical meat, fish, bread, pasta, and sweets you'd expect a canine to relish, Ferguson had a distinct affection for every kind of fruit and vegetable we could think of except for olives, pickles, citrus, rhubarb, and Swiss chard. He preferred them raw. We knew we'd opened Pandora's Box when I left the salad unattended on the kitchen counter one evening and, when I returned, found that all the lettuce had disappeared from one side of the plate. Ferguson was smiling. He had vinaigrette on his breath.

Illustration © Barbara Nussdorfer-Eblen

Having a dog as a gardening companion provides unexpected entertainment. Like the day his eyes got huge the first time he stopped rolling a warm, sun-ripened cherry tomato around with his nose and finally bit into it. Or the way he crunches up fresh string beans and limas and pieces of cucumber with abandon. Or how he has learned to pick ripe blackberries off the vine with such delicacy that he never gets a thorn in his gums. Or how he lies in the sun, patiently waiting until I drop my guard and set my basket of freshly picked vegetables down for a moment, then homes in on it and quickly dispatches the peas, pods and all. I've learned to plant enough for all of us.

We live on a farm in Maine now and there are lots more distractions for a curious canine. But on a warm day in early spring, when I first dig out the tools and set off to the garden, Ferguson is still right there beside me, coaching me along in his doggy way, napping in the sun and dreaming of good things to come.

10

My Father's Hoe

*It was not merely a tool, but a
symbol of a man's life.*

By Liberty Hyde Bailey

★　　★　　★

Either side the clock in my workroom hangs a weapon.

On one side is a fearsome musket that one of my ancestors is said to have captured in the War of the American Revolution. On the stock is crudely punctured the legend, "Samuel Mash, 1777." The bayonet and its leather sheath are still in place; I shudder to think what horrible traffic that blade may have executed. There is also the bullet-case, made of a block of wood into which two dozen holes are bored for the balls, three-fourths-inch wide and nearly three inches deep, enclosed in a crude leather case with a flap over the top and a pocket on the front. The old flint-lock and the priming-pan are yet in condition and the flint itself is in place. Empty of its contents and lacking the ramrod, this gun weighs eight and one-half pounds. It is four feet eleven inches long from muzzle to butt; it should have sent its bullet straight.

It was a hardy man that wielded this laborious firearm, in frontier days of crude equipment and of long journeys by sinking roads. Not many men could it have despatched, for it must be loaded again by the muzzle after every single discharge; the loose powder was poured in, proper wads were inserted, the great homemade bullet placed, and all rammed home with the rod; the flint was adjusted; the pan was primed; and the weapon was ready for destruction, if it did not get wet or miss fire. But this weapon, and others like it, did their work well and we in the later day enjoy the fruits of their conquest; yet it has not taught us to abolish weapons for human slaughter. I like to think that the old gun hangs on my wall as a silent monitor of yet better days.

The other side the clock hangs my father's hoe. No other object is so closely wrought into my memories; my father left it hanging in the shed before the summons overtook him to leave the farm forever and I brought it home with me that I might know it every working day.

This is not merely a hoe. It is a symbol of a man's life. One of my persistent memories is the sound of that hoe in the early morning when the lids of sleep were so slowly slowly opening, and I knew that he was in the garden and all was well. Clish, clish, clish in an even rhythmic easy subdued cadence the hoe moved up and down the rows, never chopping, never hacking, never faltering, for my father was a hoeman as another man might be a welder or a wheelwright, taking pride in the skill of his handiwork. Very smooth and even the ground was left, with a thin loose surface such as in the later sophisticated days we came to know as the earth-mulch. Six-foot-one he stood, and yet he scarcely stooped; with his right hand he grasped the handle near its end and always in the same way, with the thumb lengthwise on the wood, the four fingers clasped underneath, and the end of the stock not projecting from the back of the hand. Four inches from the end a hollow has been worn by the ball of the thumb, and underneath are furrows where the fingers grasped.

When the job was finished the hoe was cleaned and hung in its own place; no one else ever touched it. There was no proscription on it, but we would not think to use his hoe any more than to wear his shoes or his hat.

For how many years he used that hoe I do not know, but my memory does not go back to the time when it was not a part of him. In his later years, he felt that the old hoe was becoming too much worn and the handle too weak, so he hung it away and purchased another. This other hoe, much worn away, is also preserved, but is relatively a modern affair and of a different breed.

Wonderful execution the old hoe was wrought. It would be difficult to estimate how many millions of young weeds have succumbed to it; the big weeds were pulled by hand, but the little growths fell beneath its steady even march. It was a maxim with us that no weed should go to seed on the farm. And the hoe performed the acme of good and thorough surface tillage; this was its major contribution. The implement shows its service; the blade is worn to a thin plate with evenly rounded ends, three inches wide and six inches long; the handle at the shank is worn down to half its strength, and the furrows are deeply cut by grit and storm and time along the grain of the ashen wood.

Often I am tempted to contrast these two old implements, the gun and the hoe.

It must have been good material in that handle and thimble and blade. He told me that it was one of the first hoes made at the State Prison at Jackson. He came into Michigan from the Green Mountains in 1841. The farm on which I was born was taken from the wilderness about 1855, and long before that he had purchased a farm elsewhere. Recently I applied to the Warden of the Michigan State Prison for information about the beginnings of the hoe-making there. He sent me an interesting report by one of the prisoners, who has been interested in the history of the institution; and from this I learn that contracts for hoe-making there were begun as early as 1848.

My father's hoe goes back, therefore, to the beginnings of an industry, and it is a witness of all the modern developments in manufacture and in agriculture. It spans one of the significant turning-points in history, when manufacture succeeded handicraft and when farming emerged from a simple separate occupation to a commanding part in the discussions of men.

Yet, even so, a hoe is for personal and not for corporate use. I doubt whether we breed hoemen any more. Now and then I see an old man who can use a hoe with purpose and skill and with a feeling of good workmanship, but for the most part we disdain these simplicities and pride ourselves on grander things. Thereby do we miss some of the essentials and deprive ourselves of many simple means of self-expression. When I see someone using a hoe I do not catch the feeling of pride in the implement or satisfaction in the deft handling of it, quite aside from its gross usefulness in opening the ground and covering the seed.

I remember that I looked forward with pleasure to hoeing the corn, a labor that now arouses surprise. For one thing, it was escape from harder labors; and the long rows of corn invited me, with the burrows of moles and mice, the yellow-birds that nested in trees in the growing summer, and the runnels that heavy rains had cut. The odors of the corn and the ground were wholesome and pleasant. Quickly the growing corn had made a forest since planting time, and when it became head high to a boy and the tassels were in the tops, the field became a hiding place for many wild creatures and there were mysteries in the shadowed depths; we went straight into these mysteries when we hoed the corn for the last time in the season, and every fence-corner at the end of the rows was another world of interest. Father took one row and I another alongside, and patiently we went back and forth across the field, laying the pigweeds and thistles along the spaces, straightening up the lopped and broken stalks. The rows looked thankful when we had done with them. There was not much conversation; there did not need to be; there was interest all along the route; we were part of the silence of nature; but the few words I heard were full of meaning and they sank deep.

Often I am tempted to contrast these two old implements, the gun and the hoe, and to estimate their values. I reflect that the gun does not express a man's life, but is a weapon to be used on occasion, and for this one the occasion was indeed dire and heroic. Its conquests ended, it was hung away and was brought out only for display. But the hoe was a companion throughout a man's productive lifetime. It was never on parade. It did its work steadfastly and well, and no one paused to give it notice. It made no mourners. It helped to make the land better, the crops better, and the man better, and it entered into the life of a boy. If the first requisite of social service is that a man shall do his own work well, then the old hoe has been verily an implement of human welfare and there need be no apology for hanging it alongside the heirloom firelock.

Now that we are so eagerly aware of all our troubles, the hoe recalls another time; and as I look back on those cornfield days I am aware that I never heard a complaint about farming from my father. We did not think of it that way. We were farmers; it was ours to make the farm worthwhile and to be satisfied. We did not compare our lot with that of others. We went about our farming as the days came, the program being determined by the weather and the seasons. Nor do I recall laments about the weather: it will come out right in the end, we shall follow the Lord's will—this was the attitude.

Perhaps these practices and outlooks cannot develop the most skillful or productive farming, but farming was not then a competitive business. There were years of "glut," but we had not heard about "surplus." We needed little and were never in want. We had not learned to substitute machines for men. We knew nothing about "efficiency," and cost-accounting was not even in the penumbra of dreams. The men of that stripe and generation would have resented the idea that farming can be measured by money; it was too good for that.

All this is very crude and far away; but the old hoe still hangs by the clock as the days are ticked off one by one, and I am glad that it led me through the rows of corn.

"My Father's Hoe" by Liberty Hyde Bailey, from *Harvest* by Wheeler McMillen, editor, Copyright © 1964 by Wheeler McMillen. Used by permission of Dutton Signet, a division of Penguin Books USA.

Summer

11

THE JOY OF NONGARDENING

*The fun that comes when one's spouse
doesn't care for gardening.*

By Jeff Taylor

❖   ❖   ❖

Some people are born gardeners, and some are not. When representatives from these two groups meet, they slam together like magnets, for some reason. There's instant rapport:

"What kind of mulch do you like?"

"Oh, gravel, I suppose. Noisy party, isn't it? Let's go somewhere. ..."

Sometimes they marry. The born gardener brings seed catalogs on the honeymoon, and the born nongardener is told stories of the art of grubbing in the dirt to make vegetables. Far into the night, they discuss mulch and fertility.  Like vampires, born gardeners recruit fieldhands by biting their necks.

Let us proceed now from the general to the specific. My wife, Joy, is a born gardener. I like to think of myself as a born thinker, planner, and dreamer—the sort of individual scorned as useless in primitive agrarian societies. Disqualified, in other words, from participation in the gardening process. But she remembered several nameless great thinkers whose inspiration came from tilling soil, and placed me among them with a

55

phone call to the rental place. Soon I would discover that sweat, like tomatoes, also comes in quarts.

Hitched up to a one-person mechanical plow, I began my education in vegetable manufacture. Right off, I learned that it was easy to concentrate, Zen-like, on one thought only while turning a hectare of hardpan into clods. "This," I thought, "is hard work."

Later, sitting on a stump and kissing my fist like Rodin's famous statue of the pooped gardener, I lodged a formal protest. "My arms ache," I told her. "My jogging shoes are full of earth. Tell me again about the tomatoes, George."

"Skip the literary sarcasm," she said, looking over the waste-  land I had created. "Now we need manure; lots of manure, and a keen mind to run the pitchfork." All aspects of garden planning had been resolved in her mind at birth.

Slowly, our garden took shape. To my eye, it looked like loose dirt with expensive filth in it. But we worked an entire day to shape it, shoulder to shoulder. The next day, while the chiropractor worked on me from shoulder to shoulder, she planted. We spent that night discussing the little things that make a marriage, like surviving a coronary infarction and sharing the elephant liniment. The difficult part was over, she said. Now all we had to do was water and weed a few hours ever day, and relentlessly kill every insect on earth.

By the time the first greenings began to emerge, I had almost full use of my neck and shoulders again. This was a good thing, Joy assured me, because throughout recorded history great minds could always be found operating meditation sticks called "hoes." I found that killing weeds with a hoe imparted a wonderful clearness of thought. "Clearly," I thought, "this reeks." In the back of my mind, however, I saw great bunches of dew-glistened tomatoes, and chopped on.

With the passing weeks, I could see progress of some sort. Everything was a uniform green, and Joy walked among it all, happily pointing out the various good things growing. Then she came upon a slug.

Maybe you have seen violent movies, where a crazy individual maximally kills something small and helpless. It was like that. Having killed it with several karate stomps, my bride spoke of death. "Seek through the garden for these," she told me, "and kill every one you find. Set out beer traps for them, that they may drown and perish, and think evil of them all your days, nor let your hand be turned from their generations. Selah."

Perhaps many great thinkers have enjoyed murdering slugs and bugs, but I was quite content to let them live.

"But they're eating our chard," Joy said. Which brought us to our first crisis of opinion: My wife had planted many beds of debatable vegetables. Frankly, I had expected only an acre of tomatoes and three or four good-sized corn trees. Eating our chard didn't strike me as a capital crime; and anyway, I added with an airy laugh, chard should only be eaten during wartime or famine. And ditto for turnips, double ditto for squash, and definitely ditto squared for daikon radishes.

She asked me to elaborate.

"Well," I said, "let's start with chard. Its very name sounds like a term for the residue left in the waste treatment pipes of a paper mill. And it tastes exactly like it sounds."

"Oh, come on," she said.

"And turnips: Children are forced to eat them solely for the discipline and vitamins, swallowing forkfuls of back talk and gray turnip casserole. But they taste no better, 30 years later. The gun has not been invented which, when pointed at me, would cause me to suck on a turnip."

"Nonsense," she said.

"As for squash," I pointed out, "they are merely for giving away to the needy or suckers. Or you can slice 'em up, dry them, and eventually use them in compost recipes. Their orange flesh is only edible if drenched in butter and fed to the dog. They creep like kudzu over the land, their big clumsy leaves blocking daylight while their suckers strangle tomato plants."

"Give me a break," she said.

I'm happy to report that we didn't have a fight right out in the middle of the garden. That sort of thing shows no class at all. We went inside first. When we made up the next day, she apologized for calling me brain dead, and I promised not to describe certain crops as barf veggies, and the work continued.

Born nongardeners should be advised that a day of reckoning comes, spread out over several weeks. This is called "The Harvest." Fears of tomato and corn shortages prove baseless, for even a small garden in the hands of a born gardener will yield enough to feed West Bangladesh. We picked and pulled and shelled and peeled and dried and canned and blanched and froze from can't see to can't see, and still the garden upchucked more bounty. We laid in a lifetime supply of turnips and chard and squash and zucchini, enough to gag every growing child in Christendom, and still it came forth. Even Joy was concerned.

"You know what we plumb forgot? Eggplant. Next year we'll … ."

From my bed of pain and weariness, I looked up. I was eating a raw turnip, peeled like an apple. My knuckles were swollen to the size of walnuts, and my body craved the solace of the grave. I had worked like a sharecropper's horse, and so had Joy. Another year of gardening was the furthest thing from my mind. Surely there was something else we could raise. Anything else would be easier than this.

"Let's have children," I said, innocently. "Lots of them."

12

PLUMBAGO

A bad day transformed by a blue flower.

By Susan Brown

❊   ❊   ❊

Worked at the store all day. Tired. Feet hurt. Cut through the stinking alley next to the fried chicken place, skirted puddles of hosed water, sidestepped a late delivery truck unloading lettuce, onion, and tomatoes. I grumbled and growled all the way to our newly assigned parking spaces—one block away in the street behind the hardware store.

Between our two assigned spaces, there grows a tree, a stalwart Florida oak tree, veined with a strangling fig. This redoubtable tree stands not exactly in the middle of our two spaces, it is a little to the left, or sometimes to the right, and when one is overtired and backing out one's car, the tree is inclined to move. It likes to slide directly behind, and one must be very alert and look carefully at all times so as not to ram the moving tree.

This night, in no mood for games, I seriously addressed the tree, stood firmly, feet apart, arms folded, and with my eye, lined up tree and car.

I pushed into reverse, checked back, looked up front—and from the vacant lot ahead, from the junk-strewn unkempt bushy bush ahead, suddenly, into my headlights came an explosion of blue flowers.

Was this a magician's trick waved from a wand in the hardware store? Did the oak tree have an accomplice?

As if in a trance, I got out of the car and walked straight to the mass of color, disbelieving the clump of flowers growing through the wires of a thrown-down-run-over-by-a-truck-and-discarded-as-worthless fence.

Unmindful of dangers hidden in the trash, I reached through, touched the delicate flower petals, felt the sticky calyx, recognized the small close leaves. "Ah, Plumbago!" I sighed. Greed overcame me. Bending deep into the bush, I ran my hand along one stem, another and another, trying to find a root. The bush, dense with the tension of its life, had dug itself tightly into the stony ground. But at an axil, a threadlike thing yielded to my pleading hand.

I can't remember how long I stood ...

Touching the pretty bush, I was suddenly facing the spectacular mass of blue plumbago growing against the high stone walls of a house we once lived in but cannot have again. Beneath that big plumbago bush, our spaniel Gypsy is digging a cool shallow trench in which she will repose. She will do nothing all day but free her mind to lofty thoughts of dogdom, and at sundown will emerge from dreaming and innocently carry blue blossoms in her ears. I begin to see the old dog, to reach for her, so strong is the power of blue flowers upon me.

The wire fence struck me a disciplining slap.

I fingered the small root free, and with some blossoms, pulled myself out of the reverie and the parking lot bushes, stepped over the tortured fence, avoided a broken bottle, then with a somewhat aggressive gesture, tendered the blue flowers to the oak tree. The oak tree stood aside and let me pass.

There was one stop to make before I headed home. I felt better with the flowers on the seat beside me. Fatigue lifted. Traffic seemed less antagonistic. Greeted at the cleaners with an unexpected smile, I was quickly served. A customer grandly bowed me out. I was charmed. My feet no longer ached, my heart leaned more kindly toward the "public."

Illustration © Elizabeth Allegretti

It was when I changed my clothes at home I saw the violent contradiction to my sober face and shop-girl blouse; the crown of my head was adorned like that of a fairy queen—thickly spiked and netted with the jade-green leaves and sapphire jewels of blue plumbago petals.

I can't remember how long I stood dreaming lofty thoughts, but I let the flowers stay awhile. I could not pull them out, nor empty my life of their alchemy, for sometimes we are led by things like funny parking spaces, guardian trees, and old blue flowers to feel a touch of magic.

I make no apology for them.

13

THE GREEN MAN

Who is this frond-faced spirit of antiquity?

By Peter Loewer

✳   ✳   ✳

If you think Robin Hood wore green tights because of color preference or to make a Sherwood Forest fashion statement, think again. Robin wore green in homage to the Green Man.

And who, you may ask, is the Green Man? Well, first off, he's old—very old. He existed long before the Christian era and has continued to pop up with regularity over the past 2,000 years. It's only over the last hundred years or so that he has fallen into disuse, but even now, he still appears as a horticultural theme in various buildings and art objects.

In form, the Green Man first appeared as a male head looking out of a mask of leaves (usually oak). In fact, his hair and most of his face—except for the eyes, the nose, and the mouth—were made of leaves. In France the Green Man is called *la tête du feuilles* (the head of leaves), or *les feuilles* (the leaves), or *le feuillu* (the leaf man), and he has two names in Germany: *Der Grüner Mensch* or *Blattmaske* (leaf mask).

There are also representations of the Green Man with vegetation shooting from his mouth—and often from his ears and eyes—so that he resembles a character from a light-hearted horror film. He even appears as a character made entirely of vegetables (as Arcimboldo painted him), with fern fronds as hair, cheeks of apples or peaches, and a beard of rutabaga roots.

Of course, other characters of ancient times have been featured in the world of plants and regeneration in general. Adonis, for example, first joined the horticultural world when his mother, Myrrha, who was banished for an incestuous relationship with her father and in the midst of giving birth to Adonis, was changed into a myrrh tree *(Balsamea myrrha)*. Not to be outdone, Adonis himself was killed by a wild boar and from his blood, a red flower grew. In a like manner, when Daphne ran from Apollo, she begged the gods to save her and immediately was turned into a laurel tree *(Daphne laureola)*—a lesson in being specific about what you ask for. And let's not forget south of the border, where the Aztec corn god Xipe Tótec had to sacrifice his skin before a new crop could appear.

The Buddha, of course, was born as his mother clasped a tree and died amid a grove of trees. His outlook on life seems to more closely parallel that of the Green Man than the Greek or Aztec gods, for the Green Man (and Buddha) seems to have less to do with death or violence and more with cherishing the earth and what it can provide. In 1515, for example, Hans Bladung did a woodcut of a tree of life: Its trunk and main branches are a Green Man looking down with beneficence on the men below who are watering and fertilizing the roots.

One would have thought *The Oxford English Dictionary* to be font-deep in Green Men, but its comments are limited to descriptions of the Green Man as one dressed with greenery to represent a wild denizen of the woods, a character who took part in outdoor shows and masques and was sometimes called a Jack-in-the-green.

And what did the Church do with the Green Man? Apparently it wrote no encyclicals about banishment. Rather, the character was beloved and immediately adapted into the local architecture of a vast number of churches and cathedrals. There are hundreds, if not thousands, of Green Men throughout the religious buildings of England, France, and Germany.

While my wife, Jean, and I were visiting the Great Cathedral in Exeter, we saw him high on a column with grape vines galore instead of hair. On a vaulting boss at another end of that great edifice, he looks out from oak leaves in the cathedral nave. Again in a choir corbel, an angel plays a violin and supports the Coronation of the Virgin on her head, while her feet stand upon a Green Man who, instead of looking up, looks down on the worshipers assembled below. And on a single boss in the cathedral ambulatory, there is a Green Man sprouting artemesia leaves, still looking happy after almost 1,000 years.

In his book *Green Man: The Archetype of Our Oneness with the Earth* (HarperCollins, 1990), William Anderson describes many of the Green Men in Europe. Just a few examples include the great cathedral at Chârtres, where dozens of them look out upon the world, including three perched high on the south transept portal, the one in the center with a leafy mask, and the two on the sides spouting leaves from their mouths. In Rheims, two Green Men look out from the inner facade, and in Auxerre, a Green Man with a mustache of leaves supports the rafters above his head. The strangest Green Man is the one from the Chapelle de Bauffremont with his expression of the-world-is-too-much-with-me ennui; the craftiest one peers cunningly through a mass of acanthus leaves in Bamberg.

Recently, while touring Ightham Mote in Kent, we visited the manor house (built in the mid-1300s) and asked our guide if there were any Green Men in the house.

"Well, goodness gracious," she said, "nobody ever asks but, yes, there is a Green Man. Go into the great hall and high up in the vaulting you'll see his face looking down. He was thought to be a part of the world spirit cultivated by the Druids." We went and there he was, guarding the hearth with as much dignity as any churchly saint ever did.

While touring the gardens at Forde Abbey, I wandered into the house. There the rails and supports on the grand staircase were made of wooden panels, and dozens of painted Green Men looked out at the passersby from a tangled mass of dark brown and black tree branches painted in a tortuous design.

He's on the main gates to Kew Gardens, designed in the mid-1840s. And recently he arrived in our home garden, where his leafy visage looks out from a Japanese-style garden gate to the flowers and vegetables we hope will benefit from his benign presence.

So who is the Green Man? In the end, he seems not to be a pagan god or even much of a mythological character; more a symbol, an expression of being at one with nature, at one with life, and at one with the earth. Indeed, the spirit of the Green

Man is probably best represented by the lines from Andrew Marvell's poem, "The Garden":

> No white nor red was ever seen
> So amorous as this lovely green.
> Meanwhile the mind, from pleasure less,
> Withdraws into its happiness;—
> Annihilating all that's made
> To a green Thought in a green Shade—

It's a spirit that gardeners, the Green Men and Women of today, can certainly appreciate.

14

A HANDFUL OF MUD

A young boy gets caught and taught love for the soil.

By Paul W. Brand

✤   ✤   ✤

I grew up in the mountains of South India. My parents were missionaries to the tribal people of the hills. Our own life was about as simple as it could be, and as happy. There were no roads. We never saw a wheeled vehicle except on our annual visit to the plains. There were no stores, and we had no electricity and no plumbing. My sister and I ran barefoot, and we made up our own games with the trees and sticks and stones around us. Our playmates were the Indian boys and girls, and our life was much the same as theirs. We absorbed a great deal of their outlook and philosophy, even while our parents were teaching them to read and write and to use some of the tools from the West.

The villagers grew everything they ate, and rice was an important food for all of us. The problem was that rice needs flooded fields in the early stages of growth, and that there was no level ground for wet cultivation. So rice was grown all along the course of streams that ran down gentle slopes. These slopes had been patiently terraced hundreds of years before, and now every terrace was perfectly level and bordered at its lower margin by an earthen dam covered by grass. Each narrow dam served as a footpath across the lines of terraces, with a level

67

field of mud and water six inches below its upper edge and another level terrace two feet below. There were no steep or high drop-offs, so there was little danger of collapse. If the land sloped steeply in one area, then the terraces would be very narrow, perhaps only three or four feet wide. In other areas where the land sloped very little, the terraces would be very broad. Every one of the narrow earth dams followed exactly the line of the contours of the slope.

Every few feet along every grassy path were little channels cut across the top of the dam for water to trickle over to the field below. These channels were lined with grass and were blocked by a grassy sod that the farmer could easily adjust with his foot to regulate the flow of water. Since each terrace was usually owned by a different family, it was important to have some senior village elder who would decide whether one farmer was getting too much or too little of the precious water supply.

Those rice paddies were a rich soup of life. When there was plenty of water, there would be a lot of frogs and little fish. Herons and egrets would stalk through the paddy fields on their long legs and enjoy the feast of little wrigglers that they caught with unerring plunges of their long beaks. Kingfishers would swoop down with a flash of color and carry off a fish from under the beak of a heron. And not only the birds enjoyed the life of the rice paddies—we boys did too. It was there that I learned my first lesson on conservation.

Tata looked angry. "Come with me and I will show you water."

One day I was playing in the mud of a rice field with a half-dozen other little boys. We were catching frogs, racing to see who would be the first to get there. It was a wonderful way to get dirty from head to foot in the shortest possible time. But suddenly we were all scrambling to get out of the paddy. One of the boys had spotted an old man walking across the path toward us. We all knew him and called him "Tata," meaning "Grandpa." He was the keeper of the dams. He walked slowly, stooped over a bit, as though he were always looking at the ground. Old age is very much respected in India, and we boys shuffled our feet and waited in silence for what we knew was going to be a rebuke.

He came over to us and asked us what we were doing. "Catching frogs," we answered.

He stared down at the churned-up mud and flattened young rice plants in the corner where we had been playing, and I was expecting him to talk about the rice seedlings that we had spoiled. Instead he stooped and scooped up a handful of mud. "What is this?" he asked.

The biggest boy among us took the responsibility of answering for us all. "It's mud, Tata."

"Whose mud is it?" the old man asked.

"It's your mud, Tata. This is your field."

Then the old man turned and looked at the nearest of the little channels across the dam. "What do you see there, in that channel?" he asked.

"That is water, running over into the lower field," the biggest boy answered.

For the first time Tata looked angry. "Come with me and I will show you water."

We followed him a few steps along the dam, and he pointed to the next channel, where clear water was running. "That is what water looks like," he said. Then he led us back to our nearest channel, and said, "Is that water?"

We hung our heads. "No, Tata, that is mud, muddy water," the oldest boy answered. He had heard all this before and did not want to prolong the question-and-answer session, so he hurried on, "And the mud from your field is being carried away to the field below, and it will never come back, because mud always runs downhill, never up again. We are sorry, Tata, and we will never do this again."

But Tata was not ready to stop his lesson as quickly as that, so he went on to tell us that just one handful of mud would grow enough rice for one meal for one person, and it would do it twice every year for years and years into the future. "That mud flowing over the dam has given my family food every

69

year from long before I was born, and before my grandfather was born. It would have given my grandchildren food, and then given their grandchildren food forever. Now it will never feed us again. When you see mud in the channels of water, you know that life is flowing away from the mountains."

The old man walked slowly back across the path, pausing a moment to adjust with his foot the grass clod in our muddy channel so that no more water flowed through it. We were silent and uncomfortable as we went off to find some other place to play. I had gotten a dose of traditional Indian folk education that would remain with me as long as I lived. Soil was life, and every generation was responsible for preserving it for future generations.

Excerpted and condensed from "A Handful of Mud" in Wesley Granberg-Michaelson, ed., *Tending the Garden,* Wm. B. Eerdmans Publishing Co., © 1987. Used by permission.

15

Boys, Poinsettias, and Tomatoes

What do hairy tomato vines and a TV room full of kids' legs have in common?

By Diana Wells

♦   ♦   ♦

My poinsettia is cheerily blooming at last, its tissue-paper white and red contrasting nicely with the green June grass. So what if it's 80° in the shade, and there are geraniums (also red and white) in full bloom next to it?

I did everything I was supposed to do, including covering it tenderly at dusk with a black cloth, just as I used to cover the cage of the canary which eventually flew away. I even took it out of the spare bedroom when my stepson came for Thanksgiving, thus avoiding his blank look and comment, "What, not turn on the light because of a plant?"

That was when I got the first glimmer of realization that, though three of our six sons have grown and left home, I might be, once again, repeating a pattern.

"Yes," the poinsettia seems to say to me, as I potter about in my sun-hat, "I said I'd do it, but later."

I reply that other people's poinsettias bloom at Christmas.

"So what, I'm not other people's poinsettias!"

Pause. I murmur something to the effect that if you were a starving Mexican poinsettia, you'd consider yourself lucky to bloom at Christmas.

"So? You want me to go to Mexico?"

As I stagger out to the terrace, carrying the pot, trying not to trip over the baseball bats and sneakers, I think of other people's plants. Peas, for instance. Last year, I decided to do it properly for once. I marked the rows with string and planted them in a straight line. When they all emerged, like dear little compliant soldiers, I gave them nice sturdy wires to climb. I used to go out and stare at the combination, with that wonderfully relaxed feeling I occasionally get when all my children are sitting in church in their best clothes.

Complacency, of course, was rewarded, and when for some reason I omitted going to see them for a few days, it was too late. They had gone *under* the wire, across the garden, and were firmly entwined with a patch of thick weeds which I'd planned to hoe later. If I tried to extricate them, they promptly broke. So I used the wire only for hanging my sweater on when I picked peas.

For I did pick peas, lots of peas. It wasn't so much that they weren't productive, but that they *were* productive—in the most inconvenient way possible. That seems to be how it works when you're not firm.

Take the tomatoes. Every year I've ended up with a serpentine jungle of great hairy stalks through which I grope and

Illustrations © Jean Jenkins

stagger to get the fruit, now and again landing my bare foot in the wrong place, onto a hot, acidy, overripe mess. Yes, I get tomatoes, but they tell you it's easier than that.

You first decide if you want determinate or indeterminate plants. Of course, you have to be sure that the trays of determinate and indeterminate seeds don't get confused. That means labeling them, but what if you find both labels on the floor, part of a five-year-old's building project? You put them back, and hope.

Later you plant out the tomatoes and find you have far more than will fit into three neat rows. Your friends and neighbors naturally have had the sense to buy their plants from the local nursery, where they are properly labeled and about a foot high. They do not accept the little plastic cups of curling, unnamed orphans you offer them. So, are you to throw them out? You have nursed them since February, given them the whole of your dining-room table, revived them a couple of times after forgetting to water them, marveled at the way they creep obliquely in the direction of the garden, as if they knew that was their destination. They are rather small, and a little uneven, but they would not be here at all if you had not given them life. So you do not throw them out. You just plant an extra row or two, thinking one can never really have too many

tomatoes, seeing in their tiny, twisted forms row upon gleaming row of bottled spaghetti sauce. By then, of course, determinate and indeterminate have become hopelessly confused, but they do not mind. They grow and flourish, intertwine, romp, and scatter and, suddenly, everywhere you look, there are great hairy vines, stretching like boys' legs across a TV room where once you walked with ease. I know nothing of determinate and indeterminate, I only know they are determined, and each year I start again. It reminds me of when our sixth son was born: I knew he would always be beautiful, he would be creative, he would pick up his room, he would never tell me I was wrong, and, laughing, we would walk through straight rows of tomatoes together.

So, once again, my garden is planted in neat rows, and so far the chickens haven't scratched up the peas. I am trying exotic oriental vegetables this year, perhaps with the vague hope that centuries of a more disciplined culture will keep them in bounds. I picture an enchantingly diminutive garden, rather as a divorced man might picture an oriental bride. But I know in my heart it will not be so. Plants, with that unerring instinct that bends them to the light, know a sucker when they see one. They will not grow in straight rows. They will produce a marvelous crop when I am away on vacation. They will reseed themselves in my rose bed where I am too soft-hearted to pull them up.

Once again, I will decide to give the whole thing up. But then, as I pass my poinsettia, I will not pick it up and hurl it into the bushes. Who am I, anyway, to tell it to bloom at Christmas?

Sometimes I don't feel like blooming at Christmas myself.

16

READING IN THE GARDEN

Of Peacocks, Serpents, and the Jawbones of Sheep.

By Rebecca Rupp

❧   ❧   ❧

I read my first garden book surreptitiously, at the age of nine, at Girl Scout camp. Girl Scout camp, from my point of view, was not the happy and team-spirited experience portrayed on the chocolate-mint cookie boxes: The food was the sort of stuff infantry persons get in basic training: the lake was full of slimy weeds as big around as your ankle; Frisbee-sized spiders lurked in the latrines; and we were all continually rounded up and made to sing songs about togetherness, which got wearisome. I soon discovered, however, that by signing up simultaneously for Remedial Swimming and Lanyard Weaving, and appearing at neither, I could escape temporarily from togetherness and have part of each afternoon all to myself. I spent this halcyon time alternately writing anguished postcards to my parents (which they ignored) and reading everything readable in the Camp Library. Which wasn't much: The Camp Library occupied a shelf in the corner of the dining hall to the left of the upright piano, and consisted of five mildewed copies of the *Girl Scout Handbook,* a Methodist hymnal, the complete *Happy Hollisters* series (gift of an Old Scout), and *The Secret Garden* by Frances Hodgson Burnett.

Frances Hodgson Burnett, says my encyclopedia, was born in Manchester, England, in 1849, and moved to Knoxville, Tennessee, as a teenager. There she began to write novels, starting with a tearjerker about life in the coal mines, titled *That Lass o' Lowrie's*. Her biggest success was *Little Lord Fauntleroy*, published in 1886, which was all about an American boy—unhappily named Cedric—who became the heir to an English dukedom. (I read it. My grandmother had it in the parlor bookcase.) Cedric, ominously rumored to be modeled upon Ms. Burnett's own son, Vivian, was an appalling child, given to Cavalier curls, velvet knickers, and apple-polishing. He left me cold.

The Secret Garden, on the other hand, was a winner: The heroine, an orphan named Mary, was skinny, solitary, homesick, and contrary, just like me, though gloomy Misselthwaite Manor in Yorkshire—where most of the action took place—sounded positively pleasurable compared to Girl Scout camp. Mary surmounted all her difficulties by discovering—and eventually reviving—the Secret Garden, a walled rose garden, locked and abandoned under mysterious circumstances for some ten years. "I think it has been left alone so long—" mused Mary, in an optimistic moment, "that it has grown all into a lovely tangle. I think the roses have climbed and climbed and climbed until they hang from the branches and walls and creep over the ground—almost like a strange gray mist. Some of them have died but many are alive and when the summer comes there will be curtains and fountains of roses. I think the ground is full of daffodils and snowdrops and lilies and iris working their way out of the dark. Now the spring has begun—perhaps—perhaps—"

Perhaps was right on: The garden blossomed, Mary fattened up, the hypochondriac son of the Manor—bedridden and given to shrieking tantrums—got up and got well, and everybody lived happily ever after.

I read the book twice, came home from camp speaking a bastard Yorkshire dialect, and promptly planted a vast plot of zinnias in the back yard, which did pretty well. I was hooked.

Nowadays, with a vast number of garden books under my belt, I continue to harbor a sneaking liking for *The Secret Garden,* though to the cold eye of adulthood it's a little soppy in parts. It's still in print, though generally listed as appropriate for children aged 10 to 13, which means that—should you wish to purchase a copy—you have to pretend to the bookstore clerk that you have adolescent nieces or nephews. *The Secret Garden* falls solidly into the category of Impractical or Totally Irrelevant Garden Books, a genre seemingly published in smaller and smaller numbers these days—and often only available, if at all, in musty back corners of used-book shops.

> *The practical garden book is not a restful read. It eats at the conscience. It incites one immediately to weed.*

Its opposite number—the Practical Garden Book—is available in intimidating quantity and now reigns supreme. The practical garden book is the cookbook of the gardening world: a book with a purpose, dealing briskly with the harsh realities of life out there at the business end of a spade. Practical garden books are the chosen reading matter of industrious and serious-minded gardeners—a class of persons which looms large over me in guilty moments, when yellow cucumbers the size of baseball bats skulk accusingly in our pickle patch and weeds choke the asparagus. These are the gardeners who faithfully follow instructions even when it involves digging a two-foot-deep trench, the gardeners who plant at the proper time of year, and not in whatever month it happens to be when they finally remember that bag of bulbs in the tool shed. They mercilessly thin crowded seedlings, which is something weaker-minded persons are invariably squeamish about; they lay out their gardens according to logical plan, and not in the higgledy-piggledy arrangement that results from allowing children to hand you the seed packets. They weed daily. They prune things. They read about mulch, fertilizer, compost, and pest control, and I suspect they take notes.

I envy this, because—to my everlasting shame—I am not an industrious and serious-minded gardener. In our garden,

77

seed rows wander crookedly, with marigolds stuck in funny places—like exclamation points—by the children, who are fond of marigolds; we can never find the tomato stakes when we need them; and we fall heavily for splashy advertising, which seduces us into planting blue broccoli, ping-pong-ball-sized pumpkins, and gargantuan, gargoyle-like gourds of the sort seen on late-night horror shows, eating Chicago. By the time these sprout, we've inevitably lost interest and wish we'd put in more Japanese eggplants. Picking bugs off the potato plants is something everybody avoids, and weeding is talked about more frequently than done, which is how I get time to read.

Given all this, a little garden reading—of the improving and educational sort—certainly seems in order. Unfortunately, the perverse thing about *my* garden reading—becoming more apparent yearly—is that the more useful and necessary the book, and the more appropriate to our given gardening situation, the less inclined I am to read it. I suspect this is due to some large and dreadful character flaw, the same lack of moral fiber that shows up as preference for Cherry Garcia ice cream over wheat germ, an avoidance of the exercise bicycle, and a tendency to lose all pieces of paper bearing the legend "Save For Your Tax Records." I read about medieval gardens, monastic gardens, Renaissance gardens, Henry VIII's bowling green, and the Empress Josephine's roses. I find descriptions of ancient Chinese gardens—with their water-lily pond and blue-painted summerhouses—enchanting; and descriptions of Victorian gardens—with their artificial ruins and their artistically placed dead trees—hysterical. I become absorbed in George Washington's accounts of his mangel-wurzels, and in Thomas Jefferson's struggles to establish olive trees. All these gardens, you notice, are safely removed by time and distance from my own scruffy-looking backyard.

I read Francis Bacon. Francis Bacon was born in London in 1561 and died, of pneumonia, in 1626, following an out-of-doors attempt to preserve a chicken by stuffing it with snow. He was a prolific writer—it was said of him that "No man ever spoke so neatly"—and some people think that he was really

William Shakespeare. The cream of his literary works (unless, of course, he really was William Shakespeare) were his *Essays,* the forty-sixth of which is titled "On Gardening." "On Gardening" describes the ideal sixteenth-century garden, a garden quite stunningly unlike ours—a spread of some 30 acres, with the main plot "Incompassed, on all foure Sides, with a Stately Arched Hedge." Over each Arch, writes Bacon, should be erected little brick turrets, each containing a cage of birds, and between the Arches should be hung "Broad Plates of Round Coloured Glasse, gilt, for the Sunne to Play upon." Within this glittering barricade, Bacon recommended the planting of Yellow Daffadills and Dazies, French Honny-suckle, Blush Pinkes, Double white Violets, Hollyokes, and Clove Gillyflowers—but warned the gardener off the digging of "pooles," which "make the garden unwholsome and full of Flies and Frogs." Fountains are okay, however, provided the water is in Perpetual Motion. Great stuff. Also, for us, largely impossible.

I also read Thomas Tusser who, in his *Five Hundred Pointes of Good Husbandrie* (1573), cautions gardeners against the keeping of peacocks (they scratch up the seedlings) and John Parkinson who, in 1623, scorned the practice ("grosse and base") of bordering flowerbeds with the jawbones of sheep. The "Offences of Moles," I read, can be neatly dealt with by obtaining a trained weasel; and serpents, should you suffer from such, can be eliminated by "making a smoke with olde shoes burned." Louis XIV, I read to my husband—who feels we may have overstepped ourselves last year in the matter of bulbs—had 87,000 tulips planted in the Dauphin's garden at Versailles, along with 83,000 narcissus, 800 tuberoses, and 400 lilies. All of this is comfortably inapplicable to our garden, a hedgeless fraction of an acre, virtuously devoid of peacocks or sheep's jawbone—though the children, eager to obtain a trained weasel, are keeping their eyes open for the Offences of Moles.

Similarly distant from the problems of our veggie patch is another of my impractical favorites, a book much admired by nineteenth-century gardening ladies, called *Elizabeth and her*

German Garden. In it, Elizabeth—a countess with a yen for the simple life—describes the making of the garden on her estate in northern Germany. I came across an American edition of *Elizabeth* in a used-book store in Pennsylvania some years ago: a chunky little book, white stamped with gold, inscribed on the flyleaf "Carroll from Louise, Xmas '05."(It cost me $2.75.) Elizabeth's garden was planted sometime before the turn of the century, on the grounds of the immense family mansion— a convent back before the Thirty Years' War, Elizabeth tells us—located some three hours (by horse and sleigh) from the Baltic Sea. Elizabeth, of course, did not plant her endless borders and eleven flower beds with her own little green thumbs, having gardeners to perform such services for her: She writes pathetically, "In the first ecstasy of having a garden all my own, and in my burning impatience to make the waste places blossom like a rose, I did one warm Sunday in last year's April, during the servants' dinner hour, doubly secure from the gardener by the day and the dinner, slink out with a spade and a rake and feverishly dig a little piece of ground and break it up and sow surreptitious ipomaea, and run back very hot and guilty into the house and get into a chair and behind a book and look languid just in time to save my reputation."

Elizabeth, admittedly, can become a trifle tiresome—with her gardeners, her title house guests, her children's governess, her annoyingly chauvinistic husband, and her trays of tea and roasted pigeon carried out beneath the lilac trees. But her enthusiasm for tea roses, Madonna lilies, and sweet peas, and her disappointment when all the hollyhocks turned out in awful colors, are endearing. Not however, to everybody—I loaned the book a while back to a gardening friend, generally a dedicated reader of books of practical gardening advice, in hopes of luring her from the straight and narrow: She handed it back two days later, saying she had no patience with the habits of aristocrats.

Which to my mind is the crux of the matter: The aristocratic Elizabeth, planting (by proxy) her rose garden, has nothing of moment to tell me, which is a relief. It's the sort of book you read happily in the hammock, without feeling compelled to leap up and do things afterwards. Ancient gardens, aristocratic gardens, foreign gardens, are all compulsion-free. Accounts of Italian topiary, for example, never give me the nervous feeling that I should be out clipping the yew alley; descriptions of Japanese rock gardens never set me worrying about the state of the bonsai trees. Practical garden books, on the other hand, get right down to brass tacks, pointing out in precise and tactless detail just what you have left undone that you ought—weeks ago—to have done, and vice versa. Descriptions of the perfect vegetable garden (especially if accompanied by photographs) invite shaming comparisons. The practical garden books is not a restful read. It eats at the conscience. It incites one immediately to weed.

I have not, however, completely closed my mind to the lure of practical modern literature. I can, I find, read such books with absolute serenity in the dead of winter, when our garden—what remains of it—is frozen solid and three feet under; I also do well in the very early preplanting days of spring, when ambitions, like sap, run high. And, of course, should I ever prove, through countless generations of dubious ancestors, to be the heiress to a manor on the moors, surrounded by walled and secret rose gardens—in such case, I foresee turning over a whole new literary leaf. There, while dining on roast pigeon under my lilac trees and watching the Sunne Play upon the Broad Plates of Round Coloured Glasse in my hedges, I plan to read—industriously and practically—about mulch, fertilizer, compost, and pest control.

17

COWPRINTS IN THE CARROTS

The funeral service of a farm.

By Pat Stone

✻   ✻   ✻

Let's open up the bidding at 800. Who'll give me 8? Gimme 8, gimme 8. C'mon, look at that udder, fellas. Looks like milk in the ring. 800. 8 and a half, now half, now half. 75. 75. 75 now 9! Lot of power in this cow. There's a can a day in this one. 9. Gimme 9.

For me, the hardest crop is carrots. First off, you have to plant such tiny seeds then keep them wet for weeks. I do that by covering them with boards or sheets. When they finally do sprout, you've got to uncover them quick. Later you've got to yank out bunches of husky weeds without disturbing the wispy starts you are after.

And I'll tell you, it doesn't help things when you check your two-inch seedlings one morning and find baseball-sized craters in the patch. When you find cowprints in the carrots.

Look at those ribs showin', boys. They ain't pushed that one. Just put some groceries to her, that's all she needs. Give you milk rich enough to stain a glass. Who'll give me 11. 11 hundred. 11. 11. 11. 11? Sold for 10 hundred and fifty dollars. She's Georgia bound.

Just one pasture over from my garden, they've put up chairs, stage, and a barbecue stand. Spread cedar shavings to mask fresh manure. And begun selling off the herd. The Clarke's dairy is shutting down. The auctioneer slams his gavel and pulls the cord that opens the gate. Ralph Brown, the farm milker, pushes in Buffy, a three-year-old holstein he raised, fed, and milked—from birth. His wife, Shirley, a woman whose entire home is a collection of bovine knickknacks, sits in the audience, puffy-eyed, to watch.

Illustration © Anne Bessac

Tip your hats, fellas, a lady just stepped into the room. A.I. sired and bred, just look at that seam up that rear udder. I'm going to start the bidding at 12 hundred on this one. Gimme 12, lemme hear, lemme hear, lemme hear. 12? 12! 12 and a half? 13!

Last week, the cows got in my sweet corn. Three times. Chomped down half of the Silver Queen then tromped right through the carrots. Finally, I went down to the dairy barn, grabbed the barbed wire spool, and splinted the fence myself. Didn't ask them to fix it. Not this time.

The left udder's just a little unbalanced on this one, boys, but just take her like you took your wife—for better or for worse. Who'll give me six? One at a time the herd is sold. Seventy-six milking cows, thirty-eight heifers, twenty-seven calves. Then the corn choppers, the hay bailers—even the winter's crop of feed corn, still standing in the fields. In eight hours, an entire farm, six decades old, is dismantled and scattered from Florida to Wisconsin. But, hey, it's happening all over. Milk prices dropped 35 percent. Why not? When was the last time you went into a restaurant and ordered a glass of milk?

I leave the sale, go home, and try to unwind by doing a little gardening. But even here I can still hear it, a constant background murmur of the auctioneer's voice. I fill the holes in my carrot patch and prop up all the stepped-on seedlings I can save. And all the while, I listen as someone pulls up a farm, piece by piece, by its roots.

18

FLOWERS AND FRECKLE CREAM

If "True Confessions" doesn't work, try Grandpa.

By Elizabeth Ellis

●　　●　　●

When I was a kid about 12 years old, I was already as tall as I am now, and I had a *lot* of freckles. I had reached the age when I had begun to really look at myself in the mirror, and I was underwhelmed. Apparently my mother was too, because sometimes she'd look at me and shake her head and say, "You can't make a silk purse out of a sow's ear."

I had a cousin whose name was Janette Elizabeth, and Janette Elizabeth looked exactly like her name sounds. She had a waist so small that men could put their hands around it … and they did. She had waist-length naturally curly blonde hair too, but to me her unforgivable sin was that she had a flaw-less peaches-and-cream complexion. I couldn't help compar-ing myself with her and thinking that my life would be a lot different if I had beautiful skin too—skin that was all one color.

And then, in the back pages of Janette Elizabeth's *True Con-fessions* magazine, I found the answer: an advertisement for freckle-remover cream. I knew that I could afford it if I saved my money, and I did. The ad assured me the product would arrive in a "plain brown wrapper." Plain brown freckle color.

For three weeks I went to the mailbox every day precisely at the time the mail was delivered. I knew that if someone else in my family got the mail, I would never hear the end of it. Finally, after three weeks of scheduling my entire day around the mail truck's arrival, I got it: my package came.

I went to my room with it, sat on the edge of my bed, and opened it. I was sure that I was looking at a miracle. But I had gotten so worked up about the magical package that I couldn't bring myself to put the cream on. What if it didn't work?

I fell asleep that night without even trying the stuff. And when I got up the next morning and looked at my freckles in the mirror, I said, "Elizabeth, this is silly. You have to do it now!" I smeared the cream all over my body. There wasn't as much of it as I had hoped, and I could see that I was going to need a part-time job to keep me in freckle remover.

Later that day I took my hoe and went with my brother and cousins to the head of the holler to hoe tobacco, as we did nearly every day in the summer. Of course, when you stay out hoeing tobacco all day, you're not working in the shade. And there was something important I hadn't realized about freckle remover: If you wear it in the sun, it seems to have a reverse effect. Instead of developing a peaches-and-cream complexion, you just get more and darker freckles.

By the end of the day I looked as though I had leopard blood in my veins, although I didn't realize it yet. When I came back to the house, my family, knowing nothing about the freckle-remover cream, began to say things like, "I've never seen you with that many freckles before." When I saw myself in the mirror, I dissolved into tears and hid in the bathroom.

My mother called me to the dinner table, but I ignored her. When she came to the bathroom door and demanded that I come out and eat, I burst out the door and ran by her, crying. I ran out to the well house and threw myself down, and I was still sobbing when my grandfather came out to see what was wrong with me. I told him about how I'd sent for the freckle remover, and he didn't laugh—though he did suggest that one might get equally good results from burying a dead black cat when the moon was full.

It was clear that Grandpa didn't understand, so I tried to explain why I didn't want to have freckles and why I felt so inadequate when I compared my appearance with Janette Elizabeth's. He looked at me in stunned surprise, shook his head, and said, "But child, there are all kinds of flowers, and they are all beautiful." I said, "I've never seen a flower with freckles!" and ran back to my room, slamming the door.

When my mother came and knocked, I told her to go away. She started to say the kind of things that parents say at times like that, but my grandfather said, "Nancy, leave the child alone." She was a grown-up, but he was her father. So she left me alone.

I don't know where Grandpa found it. It isn't at all common in the mountains where we lived then. But I know he put it in my room because my mother told me later. I had cried myself to sleep that night, and when I opened my swollen, sticky eyes the next morning, the first thing I saw, lying on the pillow next to my head, was a tiger lily.

19

CAUGHT BY THE CANNER

Do feminists put up tomatoes?

By Janice Emily Bowers

*   *   *

> I suppose in most women the creative instinct displays itself in the planning and decoration of a house. We are not great musicians—there is no female Bach or Beethoven—nor painters—there is no Velasquez in petticoats.
>
> —*Esther Meynell*

I once believed that the sweetest words in English were the tide is out—that's when the secret world of swirling seaweed and wavering anemones is revealed to human eyes—but now I think that *vine-ripened tomatoes* comes close, maybe even surpasses them. There's nothing like that explosion of tomato flavor in the mouth, especially after the long drought of winter and spring when the only fresh tomatoes available are perfectly formed imposters so heartbreakingly anemic that you wonder if they were ever attached to a vine or whether they didn't plop out of a vending machine instead.

The first summer I grew tomatoes here in Arizona, I regarded them as treasures to be hoarded for special recipes only and parceled out judiciously to the very best of friends. Perhaps in reaction, I determined that I would have a tomato deluge the following summer. I succeeded too well. Coming back mid-June from a two-week vacation, I found ten tomatoes in the refrigerator, left there by my daughter, who had watered the garden in my absence. This seemed a reasonable harvest until I stepped out the back door and discovered that my tomato vines were collapsing under ripe fruit. Bringing tomatoes indoors a dozen at a time, it took an hour to pick them all. When I finished, the entire surface of the kitchen table was hidden by tomatoes, forty-five pounds altogether. I prided myself that, as organic tomatoes, they were worth one hundred eighty dollars at a local market. For once in my life, I had enough tomatoes to fill the big wicker laundry basket, enough to make a gallon of pizza sauce, enough to share with even casual acquaintances. Enough, too, to keep me in the kitchen for several days or more. Too late, I remembered the words of Satchel Paige, who said, "Don't look back. Something might be gaining on you." Undoubtedly he had a garden in mind.

Gardening makes homebodies of us all, and during the summer of the tomatoes I became, to my dismay, more firmly tied to my kitchen than a cat to its tail. This was the summer of the cucumbers, too, so the pressure of produce from the garden was like the surge of unruly fans at a rock concert, and I was a lone Pinkerton guard trying to hold them back. Forty-five pounds of tomatoes! How could I possibly use them all before they spoiled? I rifled my cookbooks for tomato recipes—scalloped tomatoes, baked tomatoes, pickled tomatoes, Cuban tomatoes, tomato risotto, fried green tomatoes—and, hoping that tomato cake couldn't be as bad as it sounded, discovered that it could. As I stood at the sink, slipping skins off tomatoes, then scooping out their insides, I was struck by the thought that although I refused to iron clothes, I was perfectly willing to peel and seed tomatoes. Equally amazing was the fact that I, who had never canned so much as a peach, had repaired to the hardware store where I had bought every conceivable canner accessory: jelly jars, pint jars, jar lids, a jar rack, a jar lifter, a jar wrench, and most important of all, a

Illustrations © Elizabeth Allegretti

huge enamel pot called a hot-water canner, a kettle so big that it wouldn't fit in any cupboard. As it turned out, this didn't matter because it was in use every day for most of the summer.

It didn't rest and neither did I. Daily I stood in the kitchen, seeding tomatoes, slicing cucumbers, chopping onions, dicing green peppers, salting them down, boiling them up, spooning them into the sterile jars that waited like baby birds, mouths gaping, to be filled. Daily the house was redolent of onion and spices, and my mind was redolent with memories of my mother and grandmother bottling peaches and pears. Daily the hot-water canner steamed on the stove top, lid rattling and jars clanking, as noisy as a freight train. Usually, all four stove burners were going simultaneously: one for the canner, another for sterilizing the lids and metal bands, a third for sterilizing jars, and a fourth for cooking the chili sauce or pickle brine. I savored the irony of the gardener's life: In winter, when canning would be a cozy operation, filling the chilly kitchen with welcome warmth, the garden produces naught, but in summer, when every extra degree of heat adds to the day's burdens, the garden overflows.

I hadn't subscribed to Ms. Magazine *for ten years only to end up sweating over kettles of boiling water.*

As my days became a constant round of slicing and dicing, brining and whining, I complained that there must be better things to do with my time. There were books to read, journals to fill, woodwork to paint, mountains to climb, but I could do none of it, awash as I was in a sea of tomatoes and cucumbers, going down for the third time. I told family and friends that I was "sinking into domesticity," not certain if I was joking or not, half afraid that I would sink out of sight.

That was my deepest fear: drowning in that all-too-tempting, all-too-natural, all-too-easy role. Spending my days in the kitchen and my evenings poring over cookbooks, I was catapulted backwards in time to the beginning of my first marriage twenty years before, when a really good recipe for ground beef was more precious than gold fillings and making a perfect soufflé seemed more important than achieving peace in our time. In those days I fully agreed with Esther Meynell that "women express themselves in the colour of their curtains, the placing of a table or a bowl of flowers." Scrubbing, dusting, sewing, baking, I was the perfect little wife in her perfect little life. My then father-in-law congratulated my husband on the fact that I had taken to homemaking like a duck to water. He meant it as a compliment. Even more amazing, I regarded it as one.

Sometimes I want to shake her by the shoulders, that young wife so eager to please, so devoted to the kitchen and her husband, but I should be kinder. That was all she had. Only when chopping fresh herbs, flouring a chicken breast, kneading dough, dicing onions, preparing a roux, did she feel any confidence in herself or her abilities. Only when praised for the meal on the table did she feel a sense of worth. Asked to say one positive thing about herself, it was always, "I'm a good cook."

The women's movement eventually came along and taught me to question all that—the compliments and the cooking, the perfection, and the tininess of the goals that made perfection possible. Look, it said, there are other, more interesting, lives you can lead. It suggested that, contra Meynell, perhaps there could be (or already had been!) a female Bach or Beethoven, a Velasquez in petticoats. Once stated clearly and plainly, these truths seemed self-evident. So why was I now spending every free moment in the kitchen? I hadn't subscribed to *Ms. Magazine* for ten years only to end up sweating over kettles of boiling water. Surely there was something more important to do than drag a hose around the yard and pack tomatoes into jars?

About that time, I found a bird's nest on the driveway. Gusty winds had evidently knocked it out of the palm tree. The nest had not been used yet—there were no droppings inside nor any broken eggs on the ground. It was bowl-shaped, about the size of a bread-and-butter plate, with an inner hollow not much wider than a teacup. The outer part was a thick swirl of green weeds—the upper stems of pepper grass, shepherd's purse, and London rocket—roughly twined together. Inside this was a thick layer of woolly plant material— probably cudweed—again, the upper stems only. Very fine grass fibers pressed flat made a soft lining, and the innermost layer

91

of all, only partially completed, was thistledown.

Out of curiosity, I showed it to my cat. She recognized it as something more than a clump of weeds and tugged and worried the outer layer with her teeth until I took the nest away. I couldn't let her destroy it because suddenly I, too, recognized it as something more. Standing there in the driveway with a partly finished bird's nest in my hand, I understood that we are animals and the need for a home is built into our psyches.

Convinced that nothing of value could come out of the kitchen, I had for some years turned my back on all the womanly tasks I'd learned and loved as a teenager—sewing, decorating, cooking—and with what results? The need to eat didn't go away simply because I decided I didn't like to cook. The need for a place to live didn't disappear just because I wouldn't spend time making curtains, and dusting knick-knacks. The problem is to achieve a balance.

I learned a lot that summer of the tomatoes. I learned that I never want to grow so many tomatoes again. I learned that I wouldn't drown in domesticity, I would float. I learned that homemaking is literally the creation of a home with all that implies about renewal and comfort and protection. And I learned that feminists need homes, too.

20

THE FACTS OF FRUIT

Learned the hard way.

By Erica Sanders

* * *

Sometimes teenage boys stuck their heads in the door and yelled, "How're your tomatoes? Any ripe ones?" Then they would run away, whooping. They didn't really mean tomatoes. We didn't sell tomatoes. We sold vegetable and herb starts and seeds. But our little gardening store was on the main street of town and staffed by three young women—Susan, Cindy, and myself—which, I suppose, provoked wisecracks about our tomatoes.

So that's what I first thought about when I overheard a booming male voice asking Cindy about tomatoes.

This man was serious, though. He had a face like a hero general in the movies, square and rugged. His clothes were color coordinated—even the polo shirt was starched. Most of our customers wore long skirts or blue jeans, and Birkenstocks. He looked out of place, standing straight among the dusty seed jars and bags of soil amendments slumped against the walls.

"I have just retired from business," he said. "I think I would like to turn my hand to gardening. More particularly, to growing tomatoes that are red, not sickly pink." He had thought that his wife was at fault for specially choosing pink tomatoes until, taking the shopping upon himself in his retirement, he found that there were rarely any other kind of tomatoes in the stores.

93

So, he told us, he was here to learn how to grow red tomatoes, red like they were when he was a boy. "Long, long before your time," he said to Cindy. He requisitioned a ten-foot section of his wife's flower beds on the south side of the house for the task. He had long regarded his wife's flowers as a waste of time, anyway. He intended to put any amount of effort required into developing a high-production tomato patch.

Tomatoes. Cindy sent him home with a handbook on proper soil preparation, a bag of manure, a small envelope of Big Girl tomato seeds, and our best wishes.

The man, Mr. Williams, returned occasionally over the next couple of months to purchase the best in D-handled spades from England and the gentlest of watering nozzles. Every time he came, he seemed more at home. Sometimes he sat on the squashy armchair in our library area to read up on techniques and productivity. He exclaimed over the things he learned: about pruning to achieve better fruit, about trellising  to improve air circulation and plant health. A man with an open mind, he took notes from Rudolf Steiner's biodynamic agriculture lectures on the proper moon phase for planting fruit crops.

Illustration © Jean Jenkins

One day, as he handed me a twenty-dollar bill to purchase a pair of leather gardening gloves, he looked at me and remarked, "You know, I am surprised that even my wife's flowers can grow, given the number of worms in the soil."

"Worms?" I asked, imagining the tiny nematodes that sometimes eat at roots.

"Yes," he said. "Big things, three or four inches long. Incredible. I took out as many as I could. I remember seeing worms like that when I was a boy on my walk to school."

"Oh." I stared at the bills as I made change, trying to suppress a smile. "Earthworms," I said. "They won't hurt anything. They don't eat plants."

I explained the value of earthworms and Mr. Williams listened, rubbing his forehead with a finger. He looked at his hands as he walked away, perhaps thinking of the good they had plucked out and tossed.

But this was a minor setback. The next week he set out to study earthworms, to incorporate them in his scheme of things.

In late July, he began to show some serious anxiety.

"What," he said, "is wrong with my tomato plants? They have no fruit." He studied soil types and brought his soil in to be tested. He bought kelp meal and bone meal and was careful not to overfertilize. He read books on soil science. He allowed he'd welcome a pink tomato now, even with the razzing he would get from his wife. He discussed fungi and daylight hours, soil temperatures and mini-climates. As the season closed, he felt he had the answer. We must have sold him bad seeds. Next year he would try a different variety.

We rarely saw him that winter, but in early spring he returned for soil amendments. He had developed an enormous compost pile, gathering truckloads of grass clippings and leaves from his neighbors. He bought a canner. He sent away to get his seeds from a seed house that promised the best in hardiness, flavor, and abundance. His face wore a smugness that came of reaching some pinnacle of experience in the gardening world.

But in late July, he began to worry again. The three of us would try to hide when we saw him coming. What could we say? None of us knew what was wrong (although we used to joke that his wife must be plucking the fruit for revenge). He brought us samples: deep green branches, still unwilted despite the ride in the hot car. The branches smelled strongly of tomato essence. Bright stars of yellow flowers were just beginning to burst from the tips. We held the sprigs in our hands, amazed at their vigor. "What could be wrong?" he would ask. "There is no fruit. There never is any fruit."

Susan was particularly good with him—and also slow at seeing him coming. So it was she who usually talked to him, while Cindy and I hid busily in our paperwork in the back.

One afternoon, when Susan was once again too slow to escape, she was left up front to listen and console.

"Yes," he said, "this year is the same as the last. No fruit. Do you suppose there could be another error in the seed? I put everything necessary into the soil. I have the plants trellised. I water, not too much, at the base of the plants. I pinch back the flowers to make better fruit, but still no tomatoes. Is it possible that the seed company could have made a mistake and sent me a flowering variety instead? This is very disappointing."

"A flowering variety," Susan said.

"Well, yes."

There was a moment of silence. Cindy and I looked up.

Susan took an audible breath. "Did you say you pinched back the flowers?"

"Yes, of course. Pruning the bush of all unwanted growth."

"How many of the flowers? All the flowers?"

"Why, yes," he said. Cindy and I exchanged a glance. Her face was scrunched up. There were tears in her eyes. I think in mine, too. We buried our giggles in catalogs and invoices. I heard, or maybe felt, Susan take another deep breath. Then, in very calm, even tones, she explained to the businessman about flowers and fruit.

When I felt myself able to look, I saw Mr. Williams listening quietly with one arm across his chest, rubbing his crinkled forehead with a finger as we'd seen him do so often before.

Cindy and I snorted and shuffled through our paperwork, finding so much to busy ourselves that we almost missed seeing him go out the front door. He listed slightly to one side, as though this new information had cost him his balance. In one hand he clutched a packet of sweet pea seeds as a present for his wife. A very humbled man, and a very brave man, too.

I wish, I wish, I wish him the best and reddest of tomatoes, and a long and happy laugh with his wife. When he recovers.

Fall

21

GIVE ME VALIUM

Or give me a garden.

By Anne Nelson

❋   ❋   ❋

Saturday, 8:30 A.M. The five-year-old is crying because Daddy ate up all the cookies last night. The baby has lavishly decorated his high chair and surrounding walls, ceiling, and floors with his cereal. It is warm outside, one of those fall mornings when the wind slows down, the sun heats up, and the tomatoes blossom as joyously and ephemerally as a daylily in summer.

My plan is to get the living room really clean, and then tackle the kitchen. ...

There are Duplos under the couch, behind the chair, down the hall, and in the kitchen. They clatter into their bucket and the baby comes crawling, intrigued. I set down the bucket, it makes a satisfying clack, and I get down on my stomach to fish socks and crackers out from

Illustrations © Marilynne Roach

under the TV couch. The baby squeals, dumps the Duplos all over the floor, and puts the bucket on his head.

I clamber back upright. There are Duplos under the couch, behind the chair, down the hall, and in the kitchen. I decide that they lend a festive air to the general decor, and maybe it would be better to concentrate on the kitchen.

The dishwasher door squeaks as I open it. The baby abandons the Duplo bucket and heads for the kitchen at Mach one crawl. There are few things he enjoys as much as pulling dirty dishes out of the dishwasher as I put them in.

I catch myself grinding my teeth. ...

I put the baby in the backpack, find the five-year-old his shoes, and we are down the back steps, into the world of buddleia and butterfly, asters, rudbeckias, and a few last roses, stubborn among the thorns. I weed a bit, prune a bit, cut a big bouquet of black-eyed Susans. An indistinct humming drifts up from the back fence, where big brother is making modifications to the extensive system of tunnels he dug this summer. The baby falls asleep on my back.

The sun climbs through the maples, glints off leaves as brilliant and fragile as Tiffany glass, and lifts one last hymn before the twig, and the bark, of winter.

22

A GARDEN IS TO GROW

A school volunteer gets a brat,
a disaster, and a miracle.

By Erica Sanders

❧   ❧   ❧

Children whirled in eddies around me as I stood, a tall island in a turbulent sea. Three in pink whispered behind their hands as they looked me up and down with narrowed eyes, inspecting me for flaws. I regretted the impulse that had led me to the school yard.

"What's this for, anyway?" a boy in a red baseball cap asked. For? I thought, for? What is the garden for? Gardens are for beauty. Gardens are an expression of what is peaceful, noble, and good about humanity. In this corner of the school yard I want to help you create something lovely and lasting: a children's community garden. I looked for help to the two teachers, chatting at the fringe of the group. One glanced my way, gave me an encouraging nod, and abandoned me again. They never had shown much interest in my idea, nor much faith in me, a childless volunteer from the neighborhood. They were leaving me to my fate.

"Well," I said, "it's to grow things. The garden is to grow things. We could have radishes or flowers, anything you want."

I needn't have bothered. He was already off, dancing in mock battle with a boy in a crewcut.

I slumped with relief when the bell rang, releasing me from the children and the children from me. They scattered toward the climbing structure, the tether ball, and the drinking fountain. Now was the time that the ones who wanted to garden would stay. Recesses and after lunch the ones who really wanted to be here would garden beside me, building something beautiful from soil and seeds.

No one stayed, but one: Scott Johnson.

I already knew his name, knew about him. While I had waited to ask the principal for permission to start my garden, Scott put in time on the bench across from me. Another day, after all the other kids bubbled out of the classroom and down the halls, Scott remained, sullen, for an involuntary talk with his teacher. He ripped and rolled bits of paper and stacked them like tiny cannon balls on his desk, as his teacher and I discussed my plans for the garden. He had sat alone at recess the day I removed the sod. I'd never seen him with a friend. Now here he was.

One day Scott brought a thistle. "So? You said this was a garden for kids. I'm a kid. I'll plant it if I want."

A shaggy black dog padded in from the neighborhood and stopped to sniff at my feet. "Go away!" I said, frowning.

Scott, wild wiry hair and untied shoelaces, perched on a bale of straw, spitting on a sow bug, poking it with a twig. I shot him a disapproving frown on behalf of the sow bug, and moved out of spit range. That first day I dug by myself.

The second day, I bent to place a stake at the end of a radish row. Scott swaggered up, hands in the pockets of his faded jacket, squinting. "Hey, this'll never grow," he said. But when I next glanced in his direction, Scott was digging with a trowel. Occasionally he found a worm and tossed it to the black dog sitting in the grass nearby. The dog caught each one in mid-air and chewed at it, stringy and elusive to his tongue.

The third day, Scott brought a cactus, possibly stolen from someone's yard, roots ripped and dripping dirt. I watched him plant it where I'd thought to put strawberries.

"Nice cactus," I said, doubtfully.

"It's really sharp. You'd better stay away," Scott said, making a fierce grimace.

I fussed at a newly planted marigold, pulling off a dead leaf. "Where'd you get it, a nursery?"

"What do you care? I got it from home, all right?" Scott pushed the cactus into the hole he'd dug, kicked the dirt in around it, and ran off, leaving heavy footprints through the soft soil of freshly seeded radish rows.

I yanked at another dead leaf and uprooted the marigold. "I could come to dislike you, kid," I thought.

After that, Scott brought something to plant nearly every day: a succulent with small bright pink flowers, cacti with long sharp spines, a cherry tomato seedling, and a wild rose.

"That's a weed," I said, when one day he brought a thistle.

"So? I like it." Scott set the thistle down gently, but winced as he was pricked by a spine. "You said this was a garden for kids. I'm a kid. I'll plant it if I want."

Scott did not welcome others, kids or not, in the garden. The dog was allowed to lounge in the grass and watch, but if

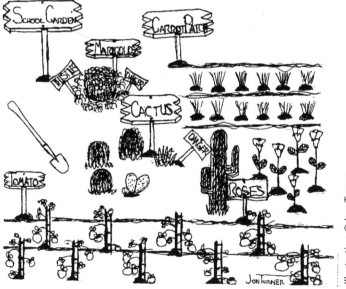

Illustration © Jon Turner

103

kids came too close, they might have to dodge a flung worm, or a dirt clod. At the least, he would yell, "Get out of here!"

One day I chided him: "The garden is for all the kids." Scott turned a dull face to me, his body held stiffly. He was hurt, I realized. He wanted to be special to me.

Stringing a trellis for peas, I watched surreptitiously as he fussed with a trowel around a small daisy he had brought. He stood abruptly and looked at me.

"See there?" he said, gesturing with the trowel. "Over there is going to be a whole row of giant sunflowers. Taller than the fence," he said, waving the trowel. He turned and pointed the trowel at me. "Bigger than you! Ha!"

I smiled. "That'll be wonderful. I can't wait to see them." Scott dropped to his knees and attacked the earth with his trowel. I turned back to my trellis, but in a minute Scott stood before me.

"I like you OK," he said, and ran off, throwing his trowel at the pile of tools.

The garden grew beautiful, cacti mingling with strawberries, daisies surrounding a rose. Thistles grew with marigolds.

A newspaper promised to take pictures and write a story.

Scott raised his eyebrows when I told him about the photographer. "They can't come in and touch nothing. Just take the picture." A couple minutes later, he glanced my way with a half-smile. "It'll be in the paper?"

We weeded diligently that day. The bell rang for Scott to go. In a last backward glance he spotted chickweed growing in the shadow of the tomato. He dashed back to pull it and fling it far into the playing field. "You look funny sitting in the dirt," he said and laughed.

"Well, you look pretty funny, too," I answered.

Scott hooted and howled and slapped his legs, hopping backward away from me, then abruptly ran off to class.

When I arrived early the day the photographer was to come, I saw Scott standing in the garden, fists by his sides, his face knotted, white hot with rage. All around him, the garden was torn up, even the cacti and the rose. Most of the cacti were kicked to pieces, their moist insides exposed. Roots of marigolds, daisies, and strawberries were spread-eagled to the sky. Through the middle of the garden ran motorcycle tracks.

Anger burned in me and blurred my vision and all I could see was the scene in my imagination: the vandals, come in the night. They must have dropped their bikes in a heap, wheels still spinning. They ripped the plants, roots snapping, from the earth, threw them at the moon, then took off again in search of new victims. I hoped it cost the vandals some pain from the thorns Scott liked so much.

Children began to assemble around the garden, curious to see what Scott would do, what explosions this would bring. But time passed and Scott just sat in the dirt, quivering and shaking with tears. The angry monster was just a sad little boy.

Scott began to dig with his hands, gently placing the plants back into the loam.

Some might be saved, if they were planted soon, before the sun burned the dew off the roots. I was jittery with the urge to help, to jump in and *fix* it for him. But how could I interrupt Scott's drama, this great grief? Maybe it was time to step back and watch.

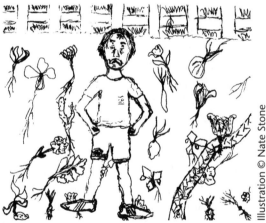

Illustration © Nate Stone

The garden had never had these kids in it when it was fine.

A little girl, Amy Brown, squatted down and picked up a daisy. Scott looked up and snatched the daisy away. A couple of petals floated down. He sat there a moment, the daisy limp in his hand. So many plants lay before him on the dirt. Slowly, Scott handed the daisy back. He dug a hole. Together they arranged the daisy in the hole and patted soil around the roots.

Amy gingerly picked up a thistle. Another child sat down, cross-legged in the dirt to dig a hole, and then another. Soon most of the children were hunched over in the garden, digging and patting and chattering. Among them, Scott gave occasional direction and advice: "Careful with that one, it has spines," and "Make the hole bigger, I think."

Watching a pair of boys work an especially large strawberry into the soil, I felt Scott's eyes on me. His face shone, a beacon over the many-colored backs of his classmates. He smiled slowly at me, and I felt a pang in my heart as I nodded back.

In a half hour, a child patted the last marigold into the earth. Dirty, with soiled knees and dresses, the children stood around their garden. They were proud. They yearned to touch, to celebrate. A hand pounded a back, dirty fingers poked here and tickled there.

Scott gave me a slapping handshake. I clasped him to me in a hug, which he accepted for a moment before wriggling away to join his classmates.

Surrounded by friends, Scott inspected his hands. A boy near Scott patted him on the back, a little too hard. Scott looked up. The boy meant no harm: he meant friendship. Awkwardly, Scott tried his arm over the boy's shoulders. Finding his arm accepted, he grinned.

A few minutes later their teachers came for them.

I was left staring at the garden. It was tattered, limp, ruined for the photographer. I didn't care. Today it was the most beautiful garden in the world.

The black dog wandered over and peed on the rose.

"Hello, dog," I said. I kneeled and put my arms around him, his fur rough against my cheek. "You know what?" He nudged his nose at me.

"A garden is to grow people."

23

THE TRADITION

Good grapes. Bad wine. Vintage story.

By Ruth Zeier

❀　　❀　　❀

In my mind's eye I can still see the grape arbor next to the old swing in our backyard. It's hard to believe that it is well over 35 years ago that I played among those vines and watched my father tend his garden. Dad grew up in a little town in Arkansas. One of the things he learned was growing grapes. His grandfather, a Frenchman, came from the Alsace Lorraine region of France and owned a small vineyard which produced wine for the family.

We lived in the city on an acre of ground. Dad cultivated almost half of the property in several types of gardens. In the huge vegetable garden he planted the city standards such as corn, peppers, squash, and tomatoes, along with country crops like potatoes, parsnips, and rutabagas. He had a zinnia garden (Mom's favorite), asparagus bed, raspberry patch, rhubarb beds, fruit trees, and, of course, his beloved grapes.

Each spring, Dad would fertilize the grapes using a special mixture from his compost pile. His compost pile had three sections, each with a different consistency. Dad once commented that half the art of gardening was in knowing the proper fertilizer to use. For his grapes he chose a dark rich blend that had been fermenting for the best part of six months.

107

He had two very long rows of trellised grapes, creating a natural arbor and tunnel for myself and friends. Oftentimes we would play for hours imagining that the vineyard was a train track or the site of a wedding chapel or even a haunted Halloween cave. There, I often observed Dad working in his garden. On late summer afternoons, we would sit under the plum tree, drink cold water and eat the last of the fresh tomatoes. During these slow, lazy times, he spoke of his childhood, his parents and grandparents, and, of course, his vines.

I can still taste the earthy quality of Dad's purple grapes. Whenever I sample local wines, I instantly recall that tiny vineyard, the small wine press, and the care with which it was all tended. One thing, though: Dad's wine was never very good. In fact, if you depended on his wine to give you a love of the grape, forget it. My mother often said that Dad's wine should have been used as a disinfectant for the bottles before filling them with something decent.

Each fall, Dad would carefully harvest his grapes. He clipped each bunch and gently laid it in the bushel basket. He then washed them and allowed them to air-dry before returning them to the press for processing. I always complained because I was the assistant and it took so much time. Why did he have to dry them? He was just going to smash them up. He explained that we used city water and he didn't want it to affect the flavor of his wine.

The fermenting process took all of the winter and most of the spring. He turned each bottle within the wine rack each week and neatly wiped off its blanket of dust. His entire vintage totaled twelve bottles. Not many, but he said that what his wine lacked in volume it made up for in taste. Often he had bottles left over from the year before. A tribute, my mother said, to the real quality of the wine.

The first bottle of the new vintage was never opened before May or June of the following year. He uncorked the bottle, spilled a small amount into a glass, and swirled it about. He held it up to the sunlight, looked at the clarity, and finally tasted it. He always proclaimed it the best vintage ever and offered glasses to all the adults present. Most of the family refused. All had at one time or another sampled Dad's wine.

Dad continued his tradition for the next five years. Then he and Mom decided to build a new home. They divided the acreage—and the beloved grapes and raspberries went with the sold-off portion. So Dad cleaned out his cellar, sold his press, and packed away his wine bottles. He put his energy into creating flower gardens and a beautiful lawn for the new home. I often found him down on his hands and knees digging out dandelions and looking over at the old place watching the grape vines deteriorate. He once offered to help the new owner tend the vines but she wasn't receptive. She finally had them torn out and replaced them with a jungle of ill-cared-for annuals.

When Dad passed away, Mom and I found his wine bottles packed away in a crate. We also found his recipe for making wine. At the bottom of the recipe was a note in Dad's Palmer-method handwriting, "As my grandpapa said to me, it is not important how the wine tastes. The importance is the tradition of making the wine."

I often think that maybe I should take out that recipe, purchase some grapes, and make the wine. I'm sure my children would find it as bothersome a task as I did, but the tradition would continue.

Then again, I think to myself, maybe I will start a new tradition: telling the story of Dad's vineyard.

24

THE STORY OF ST. FIACRE

Just who was this patron saint of gardeners?

By Peter Loewer

✝   ✝   ✝

Most noble endeavors of humankind have a patron saint, usually a man or woman who has achieved notoriety—often by torture or death—in a particular field or endeavor. In A.D. 303, for example, a woman named Barbara dwelt in Heliopolis, where she was decapitated by her father when she refused to renounce Christianity. He was thereupon consumed by lightning and she became the patron saint of firearms (if not the NRA) and all accidents from explosions involving gun powder.

In A.D. 250, St. Apollonia became the patron saint of dentistry. Because she wouldn't relinquish her faith, all her teeth were brutally removed, one by one, with a pair of pincers, and she was then burned alive.

Most patron saints have such lives.

Last month I went to a garden party and saw a sculpture of an Irish monk named St. Fiacre. The plaque below called him the patron saint of gardeners. Now I must confess that in over 25 years of gardening, I never really thought our craft had a patron saint, even though when walking through gardens and garden centers, I'd often seen statue after statue of a pious man in a cloak, identified by crude signs written in felt-tip pens as St. Francis, patron saint of gardeners.

Apparently today's concrete casters and mild-mannered growers believe that our activity's patron should be someone who had quiet thoughts and talked to birds. But I always dismissed St. Francis out of hand, since tradition would probably demand that gardening's saint either have been buried alive, mauled by a pair of oxen while tilling bottomland, or at least an earnestly dedicated grower.

And it turns out I was right. Saint Fiacre, our real saint, was a wildman of gardening, a miracle worker who bargained with the church and had problems with a witch, and the patron saint of cabdrivers, as well.

Back in Ireland in the 600's, various monks were sent to Europe to spread the word of God, among them Fiacre. Fiacre soon made a name for himself as a pious monk, but wished only to become a hermit. So the Bishop of Paris gave him a place of his own, deep in the forest and away from the monastery, where Fiacre retired to the great work of his life. He soon cleared a space in the woods and built an oratory to Our Lady and a small hut for himself. Then he began a garden. The garden, as is the wont of gardens everywhere, kept getting larger and larger.

Soon roaming hunters chanced upon the garden and were welcomed with open arms. They marveled to find such a place of plenty way out in the gloomy woods, and heard Fiacre preach and saw him heal, using medicines obtained from the wildflowers and herbs. News spread far and wide and Fiacre was forced to build another hut for the visitors and further expand his garden, and, of course, he ran out of land. So he went to the Bishop and asked for more.

The Bishop, knowing a good thing when he saw it, granted the wish, saying, "Fiacre, I will give you as much land as you can enclose with your spade in one day."

Illustrations © Jean Jenkins

111

Back to his garden went Fiacre, and taking some sticks, he surveyed the amount of land he needed and marked its boundaries, an amount far in excess of what one man could hope to enclose with a simple shovel in one day. Then he went into the oratory and prayed for help.

Now it so happened that an envious woman who lived nearby (she was probably an herbalist who, until Fiacre moved in, had advised all the peasants on their ailments and love lives) heard by the grapevine that he was up to something. So she hid in some bushes and watched the whole affair.

By the next morning, the monk's prayer was answered. All the land he had marked was now encircled by spadework. The woman went straight to the Bishop and accused Fiacre of magic. But when the Bishop saw what had happened, he called the event a miracle and proclaimed Fiacre a saint. He was so angered by the accusation of the woman, he called her a witch and denied Fiacre's oratory to all women, for all time.

Years later (I never found out if Fiacre died in the traditional grisly way or not), a great Benedictine Priory was built where the Saint had begun his solitary garden, and many wonders of healing were credited to his saintly relics. Then sometime in the 1600's, probably as a result of population pressures brought on by urban sprawl, his remains were moved to the Cathedral at Meaux. There in 1641, Anne of Austria visited the shrine. She did not enter but remained outside the grating, mindful of the legend that any woman who went inside would go blind or mad.

"Fiacre, I will give you as much land as you can enclose with your spade in one day."

Of course, with the passing of years, the misogyny of Fiacre (or at least of his shrine) has apparently been forgotten. Otherwise, many women gardeners today would be up in arms and ask that the job of patron saint be given to the same Anne of Austria for her dalliances in the garden with the Three Musketeers, or to Lucrezia Borgia for her knowledge of herbal poisons.

112

But where do taxicabs come into the story? It seems in 1648, a gentleman by the name of Sauvage started an establishment that rented carriages—the sort of small, four-wheeled coaches hung with double springs. For the business, he bought a house in the Rue St. Martin called the Hotel de St. Fiacre that had a figure of the Saint over the doorway. Soon all the coaches of Paris were called "fiacres." The drivers placed images of the Saint on their dashboards and named him their patron.

The tradition continues to this day, but judging by the taxi rides I've endured over the years, the good St. Fiacre has had far more influence on the gardeners of this world than on the taxi drivers.

This essay also appears in Peter Loewer's book *The Wild Gardener,* © 1991 by Stackpole Books.

25

SPRING FORWARD, FALL OVER

Limping across the annual gardening finish line.

By Jeff Taylor

✳ ✳ ✳

The long days stretch the neck of summer until Labor Day chops it off, and another growing season ends. But the work doesn't. At this very moment, Joy and I are lying down on the living room floor, snatching a few moments of rest before we finish canning.

One room away, the kitchen table runneth over with to-mato paraphernalia, and the stove resembles a bloody red vol-cano, oozing tomato paste down the sides. The floor and ceiling are equally spatter-dashed, reminding me of those movies where folks get their brains blown out.

Tired? I used to watch the Boston Mara-thon on TV, and always noticed that all the run-ners seemed to be wear-ing pink neckties at the

Illustrations © Jack Vaughan

finish line, their tongues lolling out and slapping against their T-shirts. That's just how I felt, ten hours ago when I was fresh. On the first joint of the smallest finger of my left hand, there seems to be one tiny muscle that isn't sore. Aside from that one, all the rippling thews of my jungle-honed body feel freshly bastinadoed.

"Olga," Joy whispers.

"Ja, Olga," I groan back.

Marriages tend to evolve their own mythology. Olga, our imaginary Swedish live-in masseuse, was invented years ago, the night we were both too tired from planting to give each other a massage. She's a big blonde bruiser, muscled like Schwarzenegger and potatoesque of face, employed by the Oxley-Taylors on private retainer; and she never gets tired. We fire her about once a week, because she also never shows up.

But calling her name from the prone position means, in marital code, "Wish someone would rub my muscles." Occasionally, one of us, wishing to earn points, will say, "Ja, I ban do it this time." Not tonight, however. We're mutually pooped.

It's been a busy summer. Look on my works, ye mighty, and despair: I have built a huge deck out in the garden, constructed stairs for said deck, installed three windows from which to view the garden, erected a privacy screen/fence to keep passing drivers from viewing the garden, built no less than seven new raised beds using four different designs, and erected a scarecrow to wave a carroty finger at passing motorists.

We also tripled our garden space, which now wouldn't fit on the deck of an aircraft carrier. Joy planted flowers everywhere, and we even got some dwarf fruit trees started.

It would be nice, at last, to stop cranking the cider press, shelling peas, canning tomatoes, and handing out zucchinis to people who visit or stop to ask directions. But—there's work to be done. Marry a gardener, and you will hear that refrain every time your hind end tries to sit down. Eventually, you become a gardener yourself, just so you can say the magic mantra.

In our early years, I tried to impress upon my wife how completely I dismissed the subject of gardening. I was happy in my ignorance. Still, when she started a garden during our first romantic summer, it was clinically interesting to see how it grew: Foosh, and there were strawberries. Spoing, and lo, there were tomatoes. Whammo, spinach came forth. It didn't look like a lot of work. Especially when I wasn't doing it. If Joy

chose to indulge her affection for the sport, okay, but the sweat on my brow was going to stay inside my pores.

Slowly, with the passing of each season, I came around. She hooked me by fanning my love for building things: here a trellis, there a planter, everywhere a raised bed, and before I knew it, old McTaylor had a half-interest in a garden. Then Joy helped me plant sunflowers—you put seeds in dirt, it seems—knowing I would respond to their growth and alien appearance with enthusiasm. "I did those," said I to everyone, "by myself."

At the beginning of every spring, we use the energy born of claustrophobia. During winter, three western states (Oregon, Oregon, and Ore—well, maybe Washington) inflict a weather whose beauty must be looked for, in the rain and cold and cloud cover. Theoretically, the days are shorter, but cooped up inside a house with a wife and child and cat and television, they seem lengthy indeed.

When the weather turns nice, your thoughts turn to the word "accomplishment." If you have a garden, you can do incredible things by scattering a thimbleful of seeds. The only catch is that you will then work all summer harder than you ever dreamed possible—and at harvest, harder than that.

"Ol-ga," I beg once more.

"She ban dead," Joy advises, barely moving her lips.

I begin to see a danger. Joy and I will lie here on the floor until morning, pretending that we're going to get up in five minutes. The following day will pass, and still we will not rise. A few weeks later, the meter reader will report an unpleasant rotting odor to the police, who will knock the door down to find two bodies on the living room floor, covered in tomato sauce. ...

"We need to get up now," I tell Joy. "Let's have a fight or something." Fairly easy to start one, when we're this tired. During last week's canning endurance test, we had a pretty good argument over whether or not it was OK to imagine the to-be-hired Olga as a slim Scandinavian beauty who preferred to work topless.

This time, Joy declines combat. "No," she says, rising to her elbows. "Let's just stand up and start moving." You first, she must mean. "If you make coffee," Joy adds, "I'll give you a back rub next month."

Which gives me sufficient encouragement to stand up. "OK," I tell her, "and if you grind the beans, I'll clean up the kitchen tomorrow."

Probably a lie, she knows, but somehow she finds the strength to join me, both of us tottering erect, hand in hand. We take tiny, reluctant steps forward, in the togetherness of fatigue and pride. Gardeners keep going. Gardeners are invincible. Gardeners do it in their sleep.

More gardening, that is.

26

ODD SIGNS

*A Nova Scotia farmer senses, in a flower,
the turning of time.*

By Jigs Gardner

☆   ☆   ☆

I was sleepier than usual this morning, which made me think about the time when we were talking about signs of spring, and someone said, "Let's write 'em down." When we compared our lists, what a surprise! They lie on the desk before me now, somewhat yellowed and smudged, but still legible. My list was quite conventional—pussy willows, returning birds, longer daylight, and so on—but the children surprised us by their observations: Of the 40 items they contributed, very few were routine, yet each one is an authentic harbinger. They remarked, for instance, that the cows and horses shed their winter coats in spring, that the horses begin to plunge through the packed snow on the logging roads, and that we see more eagles overhead then than at any other season. They saw the waning of things: hay in the loft, the firewood supply, cabbages in the sawdust pile, pond ice, apples in the cellar barrel. It was their mother, though, who noted the general change in appetite, how we all hungered for dandelions and other early fresh greens. My best observation, I thought, was our need for less sleep in the spring, but I was hooted down by those who claimed they needed more sleep.

So this morning, after my groggy awakening to the alarm, I remembered that for the last week or so, my habit of waking an hour before the alarm was a habit no longer; in fact, it

Illustrations © Elizabeth Allegretti

had disappeared. It was only of recent origin, however, dating back to last March, when spring stirred my metabolism which fall is now, in mid-August, beginning to sedate, because my body (whatever my family may think) reacts to seasonal change—surely a general truth, though it may not always be obvious when one works in a town at a 9-to-5 job. I happen to live a different sort of life, close to the natural world, so my work and much of my thinking is dominated by the seasons. If anything, the pattern of my life reinforces whatever effects the seasons may have on me directly.

Even before sleepiness, however, I note my first sign of the approaching end of summer, in late July. Driving a wagon five miles into town behind a team of horses, hauling grain or logs or sawdust, I have ample time to study the roadside flowers, and I accept the succession, from coltsfoot in April to Joe Pye weed in July, with equanimity. But suddenly, with no warning, on a dewy July morning so summery I can hardly believe I have driven this road in snow and sleet and winter darkness with the north wind at my back, suddenly I see St. Johnswort in flower and I know something I did not want to know: A pretty yellow flower standing innocently among the rank growth beside the road has quietly proclaimed the inexorable passage of time.

Why St. Johnswort should be the first flower to tell me that, I cannot say, but so it is. My reactions to the different odd signs vary considerably. For instance, St. Johnswort surprises me, but I take it pretty much in stride; plenty of time

119

left, I say, and call to the horses to get a move on, but a little later, when I see the first goldenrod or black-eyed Susan, the moment seems much grimmer to me, the difference between a *sign* and a *portent,* as it were. On the other hand, asters hardly disturb me; I am resigned to the year's fate by that time. I am not moved by cabbages ripening, nor by the reddening of the apples, nor by any other signs of the passing summer flaunted by our crops. It is the signs outside our sphere of husbandry that touch my heart. Like the soft maple halfway down the lane whose leaves turn nearly a month early, confronting me as I walk out to the mailbox, a red reproach, something bitter in it, surrounded by un-dimmed greenness.

Spring signs are eagerly sought and triumphantly displayed; fall signs are dreaded. Northern summer is so short, and there is still so much to do: the second cutting of hay in August, forage corn in September, gardens to harvest, logs to be hauled to the mill, apples to be picked, and so on and on. I resent it at first, but as the diminishing days pass and the jobs are gradually finished, I submit myself unresistingly to fall's discipline, until finally, in November when all the animals are in the stables and I'm plowing the fields, the last task, my tired body aches for the end of the constant effort, aches for the long rest of winter. Then heart and mind and soul turn indoors, just as they turned outdoors in the spring, and I am ready to sit by the warm stove and nod over a favorite book, knowing that everything—haymow, root cellar, and wood-shed—is full, and that I need fear no disturbance until I am prepared for it, by the odd signs of spring.

27

Bridal Wail

Postpone the wedding! Fred's got arborvitae!

By Nancy Riggan

❤   ❤   ❤

Fred lives in Baltimore and is the smartest guy I've ever known. We've been engaged for eight years, but I'm beginning to wonder if we'll ever get married. I don't want to imply that he's in poor health, but he does seem to be susceptible to every bacteria and virus that come along.

We had set our wedding date, eight long years ago, when a frantic call came from Fred.

"Darling, I don't want to upset you, but I've just come down with arborvitae."

"Oh, Freddie, is it serious?" I wailed.

"It's not fatal, my dear, but the doctor says it can be contagious."

"Then the wedding will have to be postponed?"

"I guess so, Pet. I'm terribly sorry."

"The main thing is for you to rest up and recover, dear. I miss you."

I had no sooner hung up the phone than I was immersed in notifying 240 households that they now had a free day next Saturday and wouldn't have to get dressed up, after all.

My Fred made a valiant recovery within weeks, so another date was set. This time I decided to forego the engraved

121

invitations and order cheaper printed ones. I sat by the phone the day before the big event, waiting for Fred's call, to say that he'd arrived in town. It came. It sounded suspiciously long distance.

"Fred!" I practically screamed. "Aren't you here in Dudsville? The rehearsal is tonight."

He croaked out a pathetic reply.

"There's been an outbreak of crownvetch, and I'm afraid I have succumbed to it."

"Fred! No! Can you at least make it through the ceremony? We can forget the honeymoon for now."

The sounds of my fiancé's coughing wafted feebly over the wires.

"I'd be there if I could, my angel, but I'm afraid that Dr. Blink has forbidden me to rise from my sickbed for anything less than a typhoon."

Two hundred and forty phone calls later, the wedding had been officially postponed again. My nerves, to say nothing of those of my poor scatterbrained mother, were shot. I sent several dozen get-well cards to my affianced invalid, who once more returned to glowing good health.

The post cards had just gone out, announcing the new date for our union, when the ringing of the telephone brought me in from Mother's rose garden. I lifted the receiver with a sense of apprehension.

"Darling?"

"Who is this?"

"It's Fred, Dearest."

Illustration © Marilynne Roach

"Oh. I mailed the cards today. Third time is the charm, they say."

"Uh, Honey Bun, I'm afraid I have some bad news for you."

"No, Fred. Don't tell me that you've caught something else."

"No, I haven't caught anything."

I breathed a sigh of relief. Too soon.

"What I have is a bad break, Sweetheart. I fell off the family gazebo and fractured both my coleus and my coreopsis. I'm afraid I won't be out of traction until after the Big Day."

Mother says I fainted, but I'm sure I just closed my eyes in a long spell of dismay. I do remember that I spent the evening checking out the newspaper ads for specials on get-well cards. Mother made some snide remark about putting her pension funds into Hallmark stock.

When Fred's breaks were healed, we kept the phone lines busy with pronouncements of our enduring attachment. With trepidation, I broached a new nuptial day, to which Frederick agreed. This time I just put an announcement of the coming event in the local paper. I'd already retired the Postal Service debt and couldn't afford any more mailings.

Yesterday the diagnosis was acute amaryllis. I don't have the heart to look at another calendar.

We'd scaled the ceremony plans down to the point where we didn't need a rehearsal. Only Fred. So on the day, I sat on the sofa, nervously eyeing the phone, daring it to ring. It didn't. The doorbell did. I rushed to the door, expecting to be hugged by my ever-loving Fred. I caught myself in time before I jumped into the arms of our ever-loving Western Union boy.

"Telegram, ma'am."

He held out both hands, one to deliver the wire, the other to pick up a tip. I gave him a quarter, then nervously slammed the door. Mother had to open the envelope. I was too edgy. She read: "CREEPING PHLOX ATTACK STOP IN INTENSIVE CARE STOP LOBELIA HEMORRHAGING STOP SORRY STOP FRED"

123

I do recall going into hysterics at that point. Fred sounded at death's door, and I felt as if widowhood were going to precede matrimony. Mother called Fred's number and left a message on his answering equipment to keep us informed. I got out my case of cheery cards. One had to do something to keep one's sanity.

Miraculously, my loved one got well. He sounded hale and hearty on the phone, my same old Fred. Should I tempt fate with a new date? A brainstorm hit.

"Fred, dear, let's elope this time. Not have a big wedding," I said. I was feeling a bit sensitive about all the postponements. My friend Ginny had tartly remarked that the wrapping on her gift was becoming quite faded.

We decided to seek out a preacher on July 12th. A load was lifted from my mind. This was no big deal, just an appointment. All would go well this time.

All would not go well. Vinca minor was discovered lurking in his pachysandra, and Fred was forced to recuperate in a convalescent home for several weeks.

In the intervening time, several other dates have gone by the wayside. Once his fuchsia swelled up to alarming proportions. Verbana brought on dizzy spells. He's had inflammation of the sumac and a broken cosmos. A spirea epidemic did not pass him by. He was hit with forsythia, clematis, and wisteria, all within a nine-month period. And I don't know how many times his columbine has been dangerously underactive.

Yesterday the diagnosis was acute amaryllis. I don't have the heart to look at another calendar.

I wonder if Fred will continue to be besieged by organisms and accidents. Perhaps I should take nurse's training. Then I'd know how to treat all of these exotic ailments.

In the meantime, I spend a lot of time sitting out in Mother's garden, just gazing into space. Plants are so comforting.

28

FATHER'S GIFT

By Nancy J. Knight

*　　*　　*

When I was 11, my parents bought their first house. Newly built, it smelled of fresh paint and sawdust in the unfinished upstairs bedroom. It was completely ours; no shadows of unknown lives in the corners or rusted car parts abandoned in the garage.

My father, an Indiana farm boy who had escaped an unhappy home at 16, was a driven perfectionist who eventually acquired, materially, things he could not have dreamed of as he hitchhiked the back roads of Kentucky and Tennessee, working odd jobs, relying on the kindness of strangers in a time when that was possible.

He was younger than I am now when he planted rhododendrons beside that dark green house. My brothers and I picked up rocks for weeks, gritty dirt stinging our eyes, brown streaking our sweaty foreheads, preparing the soil for seed. I watched every day as the pinkish red blades, thin as thread and individually countable, grew stronger, wider, transforming themselves into a celery-colored carpet that smelled sweet as chlorophyll candy. Standing beside my father on warm summer evenings while he patiently sprayed a fine mist over the new grass, smoked a Winston, sometimes drank a soda, I listened as he told a joke or occasionally a story about growing up. But mostly he gazed into the distance at something I could not see.

He let me walk on it first. Removing tennis shoes, I stepped over the string that had marked it as a lawn-to-be for weeks and tiptoed gingerly, the spiky lushness tickling my bare feet, a trail of bent grass footsteps following me to the center of the yard.

He planted bulbs after dinner: then velvety purple and yellow pansies; a rainbow of snapdragons; peppermint-striped dahlias; a magnolia tree with waxy, alien flowers; a row of raspberry bushes; spicy carnations; pungent chrysanthemums—copper, maroon, bronze— their spoon-shaped petals distinct and perfect. On an evening when summer was slipping into fall, we stood wordlessly admiring the yard blazing with color, my father humming softly, his arm loosely around my shoulders.

He gazed into the distance at something I could not see.

When I was 13, my father left. My mother, brothers, and I moved to an apartment where I lugged redwood planters onto the deck, filled them with dirt dug from an unfinished backyard, and buried my sadness with each plant I tended. Often I sat in a webbed lawn chair daydreaming beside my plants, watching automatic sprinklers douse grass and warm pavement, and one day it occurred to me that what my father had seen on the horizon all those summer evenings was himself.

When I was 30, I went back to the house on 136th. The magnolia was gone; the maple in the front yard huge. There were no chrysanthemums, no carnations, no red-and-white striped dahlias. Cracked cement painted peacock blue covered the backyard; a basketball hoop leaned at one end, the net rotted; a hot tub rested silently in a corner. The house was in disrepair, no family lived in its rooms. An apple tree, branches forming a canopy, recalled the spindly stick my father had planted to mark the grave of our devoted Brittany spaniel.

The house groaned and creaked, the wind stole leaves from the maple. As the rain began, memories eclipsed the calendar and I heard my brothers shout encouragement as I circled makeshift bases; Mister, freckles bright on his white fur, trotted up the driveway with a neighbor's three-week-old chick in his soft, retriever's mouth. He dropped it on the front step, wet and dazed, but unhurt. My mother, wearing a striped summer housedress, bright red lipstick, hair in pincurls, peered out the kitchen window. A blue-and-white Buick polished on weekends, a boat of a car with vinyl seat covers that burned our bottoms on Sundays when we drove to the Dairy Queen, was moored in the garage.

I feel peace when I dig in the ground, confident of solutions that will present themselves in the haze as I spray the pumpkin patch and raspberries. My four year old trips along behind carrying packets of seeds; she digs earnestly in the soil, pats mounds of dirt over each seed she carefully drops. In the evening, she pores over catalogs of tulip bulbs and I order dozens in shades I have never seen: lime green, black beauty, orange sherbet.

My father is retired now. When I visit him, he tells me he is happy to live in an apartment where he is not responsible for the yard. But I see him clearly, watering at dusk, mosquitoes kept at bay by an agreeable breeze, soaking his house slippers as he wanders the backyard, pinching dead blossoms, pounding stakes for lush, heavy plants.

My inheritance.

HORTICULTURAL VIRGINITY

How I lost it. The first time.

By M. L. Harper

✳   ✳   ✳

Unlike that other type of virginity, you don't lose horticultural innocence all at once. Rather than being a one-moment experience, it takes a number of seasons. (Actually, for some of us, it seems to be an ongoing experience.) Still, that "first time," incomplete though it may be, is usually the most memorable. For my husband, Andy, and me, that means the shelterbelt. ...

YEAR ONE, PART ONE

It's great to be out of the city and smog. Montana. The best part of our ten acres is the 360° view. Mountains to the west, prairie to the east and unlimited sky above. The worst part is the lack of trees—as in zero.

Andy's such a visionary: Grow a shelterbelt? Look, I'm in favor of trees, but ... . He pushes pamphlets at me. Right away I notice something about yearly cultivation. They can't be serious. We don't even own a rake.

This objection is waived aside. Unlike Andy, I know I wouldn't know a *Prunus* from a *Pinus* if it fell on my head. How in the world does he expect us to figure location, size, number, and types of trees for a full-fledged shelterbelt?

But, sigh, I do miss trees. And it's nice to read about how they attract birds and add beauty and value to your landscape. (There don't seem to be any parts about thorns, suckers, and messy fruits.) So, yes, foreplay has begun.

We (that is, he) get it planned. It goes without saying that we (he) design it wrong. The shape and size are OK, but it's split by the driveway. We don't know this now, but in four years (when the trees grow), all the snow blowing through will funnel into the drive. We'll have to spend every winter keeping the driveway drift hacked down.

That's a problem for later. For now, we order 500 trees and then have to face a basic question: How do we prepare 37,500 square feet? I feel that trying to tear up almost an acre of land isn't such a good idea. Plus where we (he) want this belt has the most sage per square inch of the entire property. I announce, therefore, that it can't be done. I suggest the brilliant idea of clearing an individual circle for each tree. This results in a "field" trip to see "real" shelterbelts—so I know not to broach the subject again.

Neighbor George is hired with his 1906 tractor and its rusty-toothed hind implement. An hour later, two sage appear listless and the sod is slightly rumpled. That's all. I don't actually clap my hands in glee, but Andy catches my "told-you" look.

A week later, when I arrive home from work, I find a road grader growling back and forth across the strip. A road grader! Mangled clumps of sage and range are piled high at its sides.

I'm not a complete convert to the idea of using a road grader to prepare land for planting. Still, I am pleased at how well we (well, he) have done. Surely, the worst is behind us.

YEAR ONE, PART TWO

We pick up the trees. I'm startled at how puny they are. I grew up in the Midwest. There, we already had plenty of trees, but if you wanted more, they came in pots or wrapped in burlap. These, though, are 500 pencil-size sticks with little roots that just lay there all exposed. How can they possibly live?

129

The first day we start planting turns out to be the last day (for a while, anyway) of civil conversation between us. It begins harmlessly enough. I'm appointed assistant. OK, I'll humor him. I try to dig a hole. I try to pick the hole. I try to (in my mind, at least) dynamite the hole. Clay soil packed with shale—it's not like any dirt I've ever seen. I finish hole number one, start number two, but he says to come back and dig more on number one. I oblige. I go re-start number two, but he says I need to dig still more on number one. More?

Finally, there're four holes, each big enough for a house foundation, so he starts planting. First, he pushes 95 percent of the dirt back in. Then he plants a stick (uh, tree), fills in the rest of the dirt, leaves water running, and moves on. I say, "Honey, if you're going to push so much dirt back in, maybe I don't need to make the holes so big." He says, "Well, sweetie, that's the best way to loosen the soil." I say this only a few dozen times, but he becomes testy. Finally, we stop speaking altogether.

This process lasts three full 12-hour days. Mostly, we're losing our virginity together, but at times one of us works alone (the other having stalked off to rummage for a suitcase).

By the last 25 trees, we tentatively resume speaking: The ordeal's about to end. Finally, weary but proud, we stand back to look. And look. We can't even see the trees. We walk toward the belt. At ten feet, it still looks like a graded road bed with scruff marks. At three feet, if you turn your head and squint, you can see ... well, twigs sticking up. What an anticlimax.

Andy next strings a wire, about 15 inches high, around the belt. (Neighbor Red said an electric fence'd ward off rabbits.) Presumably, they'd get an ear shock and be unwilling to venture in and eat our measly trees. Now, the whole thing looks like a graded road bed to nowhere—surrounded by a silly, short fence.

Like Andy and I the day we finished planting, some of our visitors keep walking closer to see what's there. They get shocked. Most are friendly about it, but neighbor Jack says we're dingbats for putting it so low and that rabbits couldn't even find our trees, let alone eat them.

YEAR TWO

A shock to see green leaves! The conifers turned sickly yellow during the winter, but they green up with spring rains. A sweet renewal, enough to sustain another round of horticultural endeavors, another lesson in losing you-know-what.

This one has to do with watering. Andy decides we should have irrigation ditches alongside the rows. He digs these: 3,500 feet of them. He applies a sound physical principle (water runs downhill), but water flows for half a ditch then meanders off. Unplanned flood irrigation is then attempted when someone forgets to turn off the water. We lose the well. I quickly remind him whose idea this shelterbelt was. Fortunately, after several dry hours, the well refills and we have water again.

Neighbor Earl suggests mulch. By a stroke of luck, ten miles to the north is a sawmill with free wood chips. We (not me) devise a labor-intensive method of mulching. I rake ridges of dirt two feet to either side of the rows. Total: 1.5 miles. Andy follows with a wheelbarrow loaded with chips from the utility trailer. It takes 20 trips to the sawmill to get enough mulch— but what a difference it makes! Weeds are down, the ground stays moist, and the graded look is banished. I sense that there may, indeed, be pleasures possible in horticultural activity.

Since the mulch wrecked the water ditches, I buy hoses and splitters. I don't like watering. How did it become my job? I thought it'd be a time for meditative reflection about the wholeness of the universe. Instead, it's dragging a hose and figuring out which stuck splitter to open, all the while weeding and throwing shale to the edge. There's no time to reflect on anything but the fact that there're still 367 trees to water.

To add insult to this mind-dulling process, the hose kinks. I shake it out and get wet, an action which also prunes branches and wedges the hose at the base of a distant tree. I stalk off to loosen it. While doing this, I back into the electric fence with my wet leg. The jolt is so exquisite that I fall back, reach out instinctively, and grab the wire with my wet hand.

This ends our bid to electrocute rabbits. Andy sells the fence to neighbor Red. I later take secret pleasure in hearing his wife complain about backing into it, butt-first, while picking strawberries.

Year Three

I'd been like a Victorian virgin who didn't know what was about to occur on her wedding night but had enough awareness to realize it might be alarming. I suppose I was dragged kicking and screaming into the horticultural bedroom, but now it's the morning after. Having lived through my initiation into this unique experience, I find it … definitely interesting. After all, you can see the trees from 200 feet away.

As a peace offering for the fence episode, Andy buys a tiller, both for cultivating the shelterbelt and for our now-planned garden. I refused to have any more road graders.

It takes Andy five hours to till the belt and he suffers total body numbness for two days after. But since it's only twice a year, this is a small price for us (this time, him) to pay.

All the Years since to the Present

We've now had 13 years of experience—resulting in 3,000 trees and three acres of cultivation strewn with perennials, annuals, even an ornamental pond. I'm awed and still unsure at how the shelterbelt experience led to all this. The little twigs are now 20-foot trees. The belt is visible from a mile away.

Looking back, I don't know if there is a painless way to begin losing horticultural virginity. Where else can you start but a place of ignorance? Still, as you come to know your land, you do learn what combinations of acts result in fulfillment. In the end, the goodness of the process communicates itself. That's the key. Then the clumsy innocence of those first efforts, which were at first a discomfort and embarrassment, become the source of a warm, humorous, and lasting memory. Like the story of our shelterbelt.

30

MANDYBERRIES

A rural Montana physician helps a girl,
and a garden, struggle for life.

By Jan Donaldson

❖   ❖   ❖

I don't remember which spring gardening season it was. I don't remember which tumor it was—an early one, when we were all scared, but optimistic. The tumors were benign. The surgeon I referred her to had to be sure to remove them completely, but then she would be OK. Mandy would be whole again, would grow into full life.

LaDonna, her mother, had extra raspberry shoots and wanted to thin the patch. We dug the plants in her yard while Mandy played a child's games, and I took them to Sweeny Creek where I was planting a huge garden. I was ambitious then—not just planting the fenced-in garden, but the gently sloping curve south of the fence down to the creek, as well. It was a good spot. The section got summer sun and was protected in winter by the small pines and the thick creekside bushes. The irrigation water from the garden would trickle through the berry patch on its way back to the creek. I planted the tender green shoots in the spring, in a staggered grouping, trying to make it both neat and random, longing for equal measure of order and spontaneity.

❖   ❖   ❖

We did a routine scan and found another tumor, on the auditory nerve, and began to understand. These were not random tumors, but a map of a hidden terrain. As each tumor was removed, another would appear, in its season. Mandy lost her childhood too soon, became a serious adolescent. Her smile remained, but her eyes were steady and thoughtful.

The first summer of the raspberries, I tended them carefully, pulling the tenacious weeds I thought I had cleared with the tiller. In reality, I had only turned the tangled root systems over into the soil, where they gathered strength, thrusting up new stronger shoots, forcing space among the raspberries, crowding the tender plants, robbing them of moisture and sunlight. The raspberries did grow taller, with many leaves and no berries. I would tear out the visible weeds and for a time the garden would be clean, neat, free of intruders. Then the underground network would surge into life again, and the cycle would continue.

❖ ❖ ❖

Microscopic tumors, hidden from our scans, would appear, on a secret timetable to which we had no access. When she lost her hearing on one side and the other auditory nerve was threatened, we searched for the expert who could perform the delicate surgery that might save her ability to hear. Deafness seemed the worst thing that could happen to her, intolerable to contemplate. She went to New York City for surgery that winter.

Snow fell on the Sweeny Creek garden, the raspberry leaves turned brown, dry, and fluttered away. Deer came into the raspberry patch and chewed the canes down to ground level, their hooves leaving deep holes in the earth. Snow fell often, covering the cane stubs deep in wintery silence, a stunted life source waiting for spring.

❖ ❖ ❖

Mandy returned from New York, deaf and partially paralyzed by tiny tumors on her spinal cord. Scars covered the raw marks of surgery. Finally, spring brought a healing of the spirit and renewed energy to get on with the task of living—in a different way. She learned to maneuver her unwieldy body and to communicate with her eyes. LaDonna translated the words of other people with her fingers into sign language that Mandy could understand. She still had her voice, now husky from the effort of breathing, and becoming over time, flat and atonal.

The raspberries pushed through the melting spring snow in several places, but the number of plants had dwindled. I worked that lower garden halfheartedly, without enough time or energy to manage that large a space. Gradually, I withdrew

Illustrations © Elizabeth Allegretti

to the fenced area, leaving the gentle slope to the stubborn grasses that had flourished there before. I lost track of the few remaining raspberry plants and, when we moved the irrigation pump to a new location, even stopped walking there.

❖   ❖   ❖

Mandy never stopped growing, but she was tired and thin, a fierce shadow of herself. Simple tasks required energy which had to be stretched tightly over her tough frame. The tumors continued to emerge, sometimes surfacing slowly, sometimes eating up space with vigor. When necessary, Mandy had more surgery to remove the obvious threat, but more tangled cells lay beneath the surface and could not be torn out. She fell asleep in the spring of 1992, and was too tired to wake up.

A year later, I wandered down to the lower garden, without purpose, stooping to look at a bright wildflower in the grass. Close to the toe of my shoe, a bright green leaf pushed out of the black, wet earth, forking off a slender furry stem. As I bent closer to identify it, I recognized a raspberry shoot, and a few inches away, another. Then I saw a third and even a fourth, scrawny canes, with a few leaves and soft spring thorns. Eaten down in winter, smothered in grasses all summer, this unthinking plant spirit was still programmed for life.

I dug the plants carefully that day, cradling them in generous shovels of earth. I planted them close to the house in a bed of rich dirt and manure, sheltered by a great burned tree log and where I could fence them from deer appetite in winter. The summer rains soaked them regularly and they grew tall and leafy, vigorous and healthy. Late in the summer, a few ivory blossoms peeked through the leaves, and by early fall we harvested a handful of berries, warm from the sun, red and sweet on the tongue.

Winter

31

LATE BLOOMER

Digging up one's self.

By Nancy H. Jordan

O   O   O

I took up gardening three years ago for one reason and one reason only: to recreate the gardens of my childhood.

It was subconscious, of course. I was aware that there was something pulling at me to get out there in the dirt, but I thought it was just a simple desire to grow things. Not true. No sooner did I bend over and scratch the soil with the hoe than I began to unearth bits and pieces … of my past. Memories forever rooted in time were clustered in my garden consciousness like potatoes, waiting, crying to be dug up.

Over there is my father who is busy broadcasting fertilizer. His back is to me and he can't see me, but I can see him. His wiry body moves down the freshly ploughed trenches with grace and ease. He thrusts his large hand in a paper sack, then flings white granules into the mounds of topsoil, deliberately, thoughtfully. Daddy knows what he's doing: he's at home here.

There's Mama, too, youthful in shorts and thongs, pressed against a massive wall of butter beans. The trailing vines hang from a zigzag pattern of twine Daddy secured between posts. "Don't pick the flats," she warns, showing me the difference between a flat pod and one that's plump, ready to be picked. Okay, I nod.

Entering the garden now is Sue, my older sister. She walks past me and ignores me, as usual, but I notice that she's carrying a salt shaker. Aha, I know where she's headed. She approaches the long row of tomato plants sagging with heavy fruit and stops to make her selection. She snaps off a huge orange-red beefsteak tomato that's split and cracked in the center. After sprinkling on salt, she sinks her teeth into the homegrown goodness. Her face says it all as a dribble of juice runs down her chin.

Way, way over there in the far corner of the garden is the grave of my pet parakeet, Petie, one of my earliest garden memories. Oh, the tears and the broken heart. It's my first experience of grief, and we all spoon dirt over his stiff form. Later that night, Sue tries to console me. "Don't cry, Nancy, Petie's in heaven now," she says.

"No, he's not, he's in the garden," I correct her.

During the last three years, when a cat and two kittens died, I instinctively knew to bury them in my garden. It was where they belonged. Beside Petie. Beside the others. My recent pets have taken their place in my garden heritage along with the animals, plants, and family members that have gone before. Alive and well, dead and gone, the images dance across the screen of my mind, then dart beneath the surface of the soil in a subconscious game of hide-and-seek.

I plant flowers and vegetables. I harvest memories—and life.

Illustration © Sandra Brooks Mathers

32

RARE COURAGE

*was called for back when new plants
didn't come from catalogues.*

By Diana Wells

*   *   *

A little boy I once knew was passionately devoted to his toy penguin and could not be parted from it. On a long journey, he was holding the penguin out of the car window when it was discovered that somewhere, perhaps miles back, its body had fallen off, leaving the child lovingly grasping one flipper. Those who have had small children can appreciate the magnitude of the disaster. These parents thought of "going back," but the journey had been from England to Scotland—hundreds of miles might be involved.

Luckily, the Scottish grandmother whom they were visiting knew exactly what to do. She went out immediately, bought a Teddy bear, and sewed the remaining flipper onto its breast. The Teddy remained with the child until (and even after) he became a man, long after the attached flipper had worn away.

Marianne North, the intrepid Victorian botanist and artist, writes in her *Recollections of a Happy Life* of a naturalist in Brazil who was surrounded by the most glorious tropical paradise and had a large collection of rare orchids, "but his chief pride was in one wretched little cherry-tree which after ten years of watching, had produced one miserable little brown cherry: He had brought the original stone from his dear native Belgium and it reminded him of home."

Winter is a time of nostalgia and, curled up by the fire, we dream of gardens, not only our own gardens in summer but, perhaps even more, gardens we have left behind. As an immigrant from England, I feel sympathy for the early American settlers who, leaving all they knew, brought with them reminders of home, often little plants or bulbs tucked into the crevices in baggage. We now know that some of these plants could become problematical in a new environment, so we are slower to introduce and exchange plants than we were. Even so, gardeners are still apt to want "rarities" rather than what surrounds them and winter garden catalogues are quick to promote them.

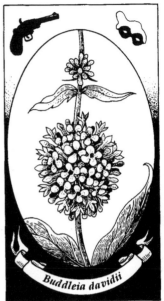

Buddleia davidii

Illustrations © Peter Loewer

This desire for the unusual is what sent our ancestors exploring all over the globe for exciting introductions. Their trips were not gentle botanizing but real adventure. The list of botanists who risked or even lost their lives to bring back plants is a long one. Attacks from natives, cold, and hunger were constant threats. In the warmth of our living rooms, with catalogues of the hundreds of plants now available, it is amazing to think of what they did, and why.

Plant explorers were not ordinary travellers, even when travelling itself was not easy. They had to carry everything they needed into remote, inaccessible areas. This included pens and inkhorns to make notes and reams of heavy paper for pressing specimens. Seeds and plants had to be prevented from rotting and yet not dry out. There was little room left for clothing, comforts, or even food. They lived off the land as they could.

David Douglas, who first brought so many of our plants from the West Coast, describes rats eating his shoes and ink-case. When he got soaked, which was often, he simply took his clothes off and sat by the fire. He once had to eat all his collection of seeds and, later, even his horse. He pacified hostile Indians by giving them the buttons off his coat.

Linnaeus's luggage was similar. It included ink and paper, a magnifying glass, his manuscripts on ornithology and flora, but only one extra shirt, two night caps, and two "half-sleeves" in the way of clothing. Explorers often slept on the open ground with no tents—William Bartram describes waking up to find an alligator's open mouth a few feet away from him. Luckily, he was able to stay awake the rest of the night, helped by biting mosquitoes and owl cries vibrating through the forests "in dreadful peals."

It's easy enough for us to order plants that were introduced after such adventures. Sometimes going round my garden, I think of what it took to get them there. Forsythia makes me think of Robert Fortune sneaking into the forbidden interior of China wearing a false pigtail. A Regal lily in bloom makes

Wisteria floribunda

me thank Ernest Wilson, lying on his back on a narrow mountain pass while forty mules going the other way stepped over his rockslide-shattered leg. John Bannister, who found the beautiful bloodroot and Virginia bluebell, both of which I have in abundance, fell off a cliff while botanizing and died. The *Cunninghamia* by our pond, an evergreen from China with foliage not unlike that of a monkey-puzzle, was named for James Cunningham, who was the only survivor of a massacre and was later both wounded and imprisoned. He eventually died at sea. My *Buddleia davidii*, often covered with butterflies, was first sent back by Jean André Soulié, who was killed by bandits. George Forrest collected the ancestors of many of our rhododendron. He narrowly escaped being massacred in Tibet by rolling off a path into the jungle and hiding there with no food but a handful of peas and without even his boots, which he removed to prevent being tracked. I have Japanese wisteria and the "PG" hydrangea—both introduced by Jean Siebold. He performed the first cataract operations in Japan where, in exchange for restoring sight, he would be given new plant specimens. He was finally imprisoned and barely pardoned for obtaining a map of Japan at a time when that was a capital offense for foreigners. I sometimes plant "poached egg plant" to attract bees—and think of David Douglas when it flowers. I have a particular affection for Douglas, not only because of the many plants he introduced (including, of course, the Douglas fir), but also because he wore a suit of flamboyant Stuart tartan in the remotest wilderness in case he should come across fellow Scottish travellers. He died in Hawaii by falling into a bull pit while botanizing. I don't grow saffron crocus but do use it in cooking, while thinking of the legend-

Jean Siebold, who performed the first cata- ract operations in Japan, was imprisoned.

ary pilgrim who brought it back hidden in his hollowed-out staff, "for if he had bene taken ... he had died for the fact."

When we order from catalogues, we expect plants to arrive in prime condition and, if they do not, are quick to demand replacements. In the past, attempts to send hard-won plants home intact were more often unsuccessful than not. This added to the quantities collected—quantities which now horrify us—for most could not be expected to reach their destination.

Plant explorers of the past searched as ardently for ways of keeping their finds alive as they did to acquire them. Bernard Jussieu was said to have brought the first Cedar of Lebanon back to Paris in his own hat and to have shared his water ration with it. Peter Collinson, who received seeds and plants from John Bartram, was always writing with new suggestions to protect specimens—such as using ox bladders to contain the earth-packed roots of a plant while the rest, tightly bound, would stick out of the neck. Linnaeus advocated putting seeds into a bottle of sand and placing that bottle into a bigger one, which was, in turn, filled with a mixture of nitre, salt, and sal ammonia. John Evelyn suggested that "plants or rootes that come from abroad will be better preserved if they are rubbed over with honey before they are covered with moss" for "honey has a styptic quality to hinder the moisting that is in the plants from perspiring." Sometimes seeds would be covered with bees-wax or lard, then wrapped in arsenic-soaked paper to protect them from mice and rats.

David Douglas died while botanizing in Hawaii. He fell into a bull pit.

The invention of the glass Wardian case in 1834 considerably improved the chances of plant survival. This airtight case protected the contents from salt air and maintained a constant damp atmosphere. If created earlier, it might have helped protect some plants from more than salt: The arrangements for transporting the breadfruit plants on the Bounty in 1787 had meant sacrificing both cabin space and fresh water to them—factors in the famous mutiny. (That mutiny caused the death of yet another botanist, Nelson, who was set adrift with Captain Bligh and died before reaching home.)

Several sea captains had a small business in transporting plants like the first "tea roses," which came along with tea shipments from China. Sailors, too, probably brought many plants back from abroad. They're known to have planted anti-scorbic plants like citrus and rhubarb wherever ships called routinely. There is a nice story that the Fuchsia was first brought to England by a sailor as a present to his mother. It was then spotted on a windowsill by the nurseryman Lee, who, unable to persuade her to part with it, "borrowed" it from her for eight guineas and propagated it.

Even with so many plants to choose from, the word "rare" immediately catches my eye, as it has for gardeners always. Peter Collinson wrote disarmingly to John Bartram that he was "ready to Burst with Desire for Root, Seed or Specimen of the Wagish Tipitwitchet Sensitive." All of us know the pleasure of showing a neighbour an unusual plant we have managed to raise. Most of us are less ingenuous than Peter Collinson, 145 firmly but casually leading our visitor to the spot next to the plant we wish to show off. Real friends will immediately ask about the plant they do not recognize (those who do not ask are probably not real friends and can be discounted). Then we remark blithely, "Oh, that? Yes, I'm quite pleased with it. It's a Pseudo vanitas erectus, and it's the first time I've tried it. I wanted to see if the flowers were *really* green. ..."

I might try a little subterfuge to draw attention to a rarity of mine, but sometimes plant collectors of the past were outright dishonest. In the early seventeenth century, a Monsieur Bachelier had some anemone plants from the Middle East which he would not share with any other collectors. He was finally outwitted by a Dutch Councillor of Parliament, who visited the garden and "accidentally" dropped his fur cloak on the border where the anemones were growing. His servant, primed beforehand, scooped up the cloak and, with it, some adhering seeds. The plants grown from these were known as "French" anemones.

Another collector, the Duke of Devonshire, along with his famous gardener Paxton (who was the first to bring the *Victoria amazonica* to flower and designed the Crystal Palace) was so keen to have the first *Amherstia nobilis* that the Duke hired John Gibson to go to India and bring one home. Hortus describes the *Amherstia* as "one of the noblest flowering trees" and, to add to its attraction, it had hardly ever been seen in the wild but was discovered in a neglected monastery garden. Gibson did find one and was described as running round it "clapping his hands like a boy who has got three runs in a cricket match." The tree destined for the Duke of Devonshire died on the voyage home, but there was another on board which was a present from the Director of the Botanic Gardens in Calcutta to the Directors of the East India Company in

London. This plant was met by Paxton and whisked down to the Duke's estate at Chatsworth by a special fast canal boat. The Duke then wrote to the Directors of the East India Company, "It was necessary to remove the plant from the ship—I shall, however, be most ready to return the *Amherstia* whenever you demand me to do so." Needless to say, the *Amherstia* stayed at Chatsworth!

I love the passion of these plant collectors and wonder if, with so much available, we aren't a little jaded these days. Not much notice is taken now when new plants are discovered. Compare this with the introduction in 1788 of the *Hydrangea hortensis*. Ernest Wilson wrote about its arrival in London: "It was met on the docks by a delegation of plant enthusiasts and patrons of horticulture, including Sir Joseph Banks. After the ceremony attending the plant's arrival and inspection, a breakfast in its honor was given."

I have two hydrangeas, and I put aluminum sulphate around them to make their blooms a brilliant, unrealistic sky blue. I sometimes have my own breakfast on the terrace next to them. Once they were in bloom beside an arch covered with Heavenly Blue morning glories, whose breathtaking show lasts only a few hours. For that moment, I was perhaps worthy of the sacrifices and triumphs of those plant hunters of the past, because I decided to have, if not a breakfast, at least a viewing in the plants' honor. It was 6:30 A.M., but I had one friend whom I knew I could call.

"Come right over and see something beautiful," I said. With true plant-lover's passion, she came.

33

THE OCCASIONAL GARDEN

*For those times when you're planning a party and
need a perfect garden—tomorrow.*

By Saki

❁   ❁   ❁

"Don't talk to me about town gardens," said Elinor Rapsley;
"which means, of course, that I want you to listen to me for
an hour or so while I talk about nothing else. 'What a nice-
sized garden you've got,' people said to us when we first moved
here. What I suppose they meant to say was what a nice-sized
site for a garden we'd got. As a matter of fact, the size is all
against it; it's too large to be ignored altogether and treated as
a yard, and it's too small to keep giraffes in. You see, if we
could keep giraffes or reindeer or some other species of brows-
ing animal there we could explain the general absence of vegetation by a reference to the fauna of the garden: 'You can't
have wapiti and Darwin tulips, you know, so we didn't put
down any bulbs last year.' As it is, we haven't got the wapiti,
and the Darwin tulips haven't survived the fact that most of
the cats of the neighborhood hold a parliament in the center
of the tulip bed; that rather forlorn-looking strip that we intended to be a border of alternating geranium and spiraea has
been utilized by the cat-parliament as a division lobby. Snap
divisions seem to have been rather frequent of late, far more
frequent than the geranium blooms are likely to be. I shouldn't
object so much to ordinary cats, but I do complain of having

a congress of vegetarian cats in my garden; they must be vegetarians, my dear, because, whatever ravages they may commit among the sweet-pea seedlings, they never seem to touch the sparrows; there are always just as many adult sparrows in the garden on Saturday as there were on Monday, not to mention newly fledged additions. There seems to have been an irreconcilable difference of opinion between sparrows and Providence since the beginning of time as to whether a crocus looks best standing upright with its roots in the earth or in a recumbent posture with its stem neatly severed; the sparrows always have the last word in the matter, at least in our garden they do. I fancy that Providence must have originally intended to bring in an amending *Suppose you have* Act, or whatever it's called, providing either *people coming to* for less destructive sparrow or a more inde- *lunch at one-* structible crocus. The one consoling point *thirty; you just* about our garden is that it's not visible from *ring up the Asso-* the drawing room or the smoking room, so *ciation at about* unless people are dining or lunching with us *ten and say,* they can't spy out the nakedness of the land. *"Lunch garden."* That is why I am so furious with Gwenda Pottingdon, who has practically forced herself on me for lunch on Wednesday next; she heard me offer the Paulcote girl lunch if she was up shopping on that day, and, of course, she asked if she might come too. She is only coming to gloat over my bedraggled and flowerless borders and to sing the praises of her own detestably over cultivated garden. I'm sick of being told it's the envy of the neighborhood; it's like everything else that belongs to her—her car, her dinner parties, even her headaches, they are all superlative; no one else ever had anything like them. When her eldest child was confirmed it was such a sensational event, according to her account of it, that one almost expected questions to be asked about it in the House of Commons, and now she's coming on purpose to stare at my few miserable pansies and the gaps in my sweet pea border, and to give me a glowing, full-length description of the rare and sumptuous blooms in her rose garden."

149

Illustrations © Derek Collins

"My dear Elinor," said the Baroness, "you would save your-self all this heartburning and a lot of gardener's bills, not to mention sparrow anxieties, simply by paying an annual sub-scription to the O.O.S.A."

"Never heard of it," said Elinor; "what is it?"

"The Occasional-Oasis Supply Association," said the Baroness; "it exists to meet cases exactly like yours, cases of backyards that are of no practical use for gardening purposes, but are required to blossom into decorative scenic backgrounds at stated intervals, when a luncheon or dinner party is   151 contemplated. Supposing, for instance, you have people coming to lunch at one-thirty; you just ring up the Association at about ten o'clock the same morning and say, 'Lunch garden.' That is all the trouble you have to take. By twelve forty-five your yard is carpeted with a strip of velvety turf, with a hedge of lilac or red may, whatever happens to be in season, as a background, one or two cherry tress in blossom, and clumps of heavily flowered rhododendrons filling in the odd corners; in the foreground you have a blaze of carnations or Shirley poppies, or tiger lilies in full bloom. As soon as the lunch is over and your guests have departed the garden departs also, and all the cats in Christendom can sit in council in your yard without causing you a moment's anxiety. If you have a bishop or an antiquary or something of that sort coming to lunch you just mention the fact when you are ordering the garden, and you get an old world pleasaunce, with clipped yew hedges and a sundial and hollyhocks, and perhaps a mulberry tree, and borders of sweet williams and Canterbury bells, and an old-fashioned beehive or two tucked away in a corner. Those are the ordinary lines of supply that the Oasis Association undertakes, but by paying a few guineas a year extra you are entitled to its emergency E.O.N. service."

> *Gwenda Pottingdon did not enjoy her lunch; the piquant sauce of her own conversation was notably lacking.*

"What on earth is E.O.N. service?"

"It's just like a conventional signal to indicate special cases like the incursion of Gwenda Pottingdon. It means you've got someone coming to lunch or dinner whose garden is alleged to be 'the envy of the neighborhood.'"

"Yes," exclaimed Elinor, with some excitement, "and what happens then?"

"Something that sounds like a miracle out of the Arabian Nights. Your backyard becomes voluptuous with pomegranate and almond trees, lemon groves, and hedges of flowering cactus, dazzling banks of azaleas, marble-basin fountains, in which chestnut-and-white pond-herons step daintily amid exotic water lilies, while golden pheasants strut about on alabaster terraces. The whole effect rather suggests the background for an open air Russian Ballet; in point of fact, it is merely the background to your luncheon party. If there is any kick left in Gwenda Pottingdon, or whoever your E.O.N. guest of the moment may be, just mention carelessly that your climbing putella is the only one in England, since the one at Chatsworth died last winter. There isn't such a thing as a climbing putella, but Gwenda Pottingdon and her kind don't usually know one flower from another without prompting."

"Quick," said Elinor, "the address of the Association."

Gwenda Pottingdon did not enjoy her lunch. It was a simple yet elegant meal, excellently cooked and daintily served, but the piquant sauce of her own conversation was notably lacking. She had prepared a long succession of eulogistic comments on the wonders of her town garden, with its unrivaled effects of horticultural magnificence, and, behold, her theme was shut in on every side by the luxuriant hedge of Siberian berberis that formed a glowing background to Elinor's bewildering fragment of fairyland. The pomegranate and lemon trees, the terraced fountain, where gold carp slithered and wriggled amid the roots of gorgeous-hued irises, the banked masses of exotic blooms, the pagoda-like enclosure, where Japanese sandbadgers disported themselves, all these contributed to take away Gwenda's appetite and moderate her desire to talk about gardening matters.

"I can't say I admire the climbing putella," she observed shortly, "and anyway it's not the only one of its kind in England; I happen to know of one in Hampshire. How gardening is going out of fashion. I suppose people haven't the time for it nowadays."

Altogether it was quite one of Elinor's most successful luncheon parties.

It was distinctly an unforeseen catastrophe that Gwenda should have burst in on the household four days later at lunchtime and made her way unbidden into the dining room.

153

"I thought I must tell you that my Elaine has had a water-color sketch accepted by the Latent Talent Art Guild; it's to be exhibited at their summer exhibition at the Hackney Gallery. It will be the sensation of the moment in the art world—Hullo, what on earth happened to your garden? It's not there!"

"Suffragettes," said Elinor promptly; "didn't you hear about it? They broke in and made hay of the whole thing in about ten minutes. I was so heartbroken at the havoc that I had the whole place cleared out; I shall have it laid out again on rather more elaborate lines."

"That," she said to the Baroness afterwards, "is what I call having an emergency brain."

From *The Complete Short Stories of Saki* by H. H. Munro. Courtesy of Penguin USA.

34

HUNTING A CHRISTMAS TREE

In taking life, she harvested truth.

By Barbara Dean

❄   ❄   ❄

I am late for everything. It's December 23rd and although the solstice has come and gone, not a single fir bough drapes the window ledges. The press of last-minute work has delayed my usual preparations—but this weekend I will catch up. Throughout a busy week, I have aimed myself toward this day, which I have set aside for getting my Christmas tree.

The morning is overcast, the temperature unusually cold for northern California. In the meadow, the night's frost still clings to the dead stalks of last spring's grass. Calling for Nandi, my Rhodesian Ridgeback who is always ready for adventure, I reach for my jacket, gloves, and then the bow saw that hangs from a nail on the outside back wall of my house. She follows my cue, as I move toward the cold side of the gentle slope to the north of the house.

Despite my love for Christmas, cutting a tree is always a daunting project. This square mile of remote mountain land was logged almost thirty years ago, and although it is important to me that my Christmas tree come from this place that has become the ground of my life, I also want the second-growth forest to flourish. So I must find a tree in a group that needs thinning or one that has started in such poor soil that I

Illustrations © Elizabeth Allegretti

doubt it will thrive. The problem, of course, with choosing a tree from a close-growing group is that nearly always it is also scrawny or lopsided. Wild trees don't have the groomed fullness and symmetry of those in Christmas tree farms.

And yet I want a tree that comes close to my perfect vision from childhood. Each year, as I walk over the land in the months before Christmas, I make mental notes of the young

Douglas firs. This fall my wanderings have led me again and again to the tree we are walking toward today, a tree that I have watched for years. The tree is about the right height—six feet—and about the right diameter, as far as I can tell. The deer have browsed the branches, a natural pruning that helps them to grow full. Most important, the trunk of this tree grows only two feet from the trunk of another.

As I have passed the tree in the last months, I have been nodding to it, getting to know it, measuring it in my mind's eye for its spot in my house. The years of watching it grow have established a familiarity between us, at least on my part. I have visited this tree during summer's searing heat, on fall days when mist hung in the air, and in the frosted quiet of winter. I have felt the tree's prickly needles, circled its small gray trunk with my hands. This tree and I have been neighbors: the same winds that have rustled its needles have blown through my hair; I know the deer who have browsed its branches; the same wary bobcat, brilliant hummingbirds, and family of raccoons have encountered us both.

After so much time and shared experience, I have a particular feeling for this particular tree—and here is where the difficulty is. For I am about to kill it.

At times like this, I wonder whether living in this near-wilderness has rendered me unfit for twentieth-century life. When I was a child, Christmas tree-cutting adventures with my family were a high point of the season; we children would race around the hill, choosing the "best" tree, always wanting Dad to cut the biggest. I don't remember that the scruples I struggle with now were any part of those days.

But years of living in this wild place have changed me in ways that I could not reverse even if I wanted to. Among the changes, those pressing on me today are an awareness of the individual essence of this tree and the terrible knowledge that all life depends on death.

I am not planning to eat this tree, of course. Rather than feeding my body, the tree will feed my soul. But the distinction blurs. The central paradox, the truth that is at the heart of all life on earth, remains.

I have been a vegetarian for more than twenty years, which I once thought exempted me from the violence that accompanies the securing of food. But a few weeks of working in the garden my first summer here—weeding, transplanting, thinning, harvesting—did away with that comforting illusion. Picking a blackberry may not kill the bush, but what about pulling up a carrot? Besides, I soon grew uncomfortable with the notion that even a berry might not have a life.

> *I have a particular feeling for this particular tree—and here is where the difficulty is. For I am about to kill it.*

Each death is clearly part of sustaining another life, and, just as clearly, my own survival depends on being part of this chain every day in one way or another. Most of the time, I understand this inescapable reality well enough to justify my own role. But sometimes the darkness at the heart of that logic breaks through, and I face what seems an intolerable truth.

Perhaps it is because of Christmas, because of the feeling of ceremony that hovers in the air, because of the season's unusually fragile veil between spirit and nature—whatever the reason, today my killing of this tree seems to epitomize my life's dependence on the death of another life. Today this seems to me a profound and chilling mystery, not easily accommodated in the soul. And nothing in my own upbringing has taught me how to make peace with it.

Soon after moving to the country, the intensity of my feelings for this land caught me by surprise. Looking for insight, I sought out books about the Native Americans who first lived in these hills, and then about other cultural groups that lived close to the earth, reaching back to the earliest hunter-gatherers. Something compelled me to read about the experience of the hunt, and to explore as much as possible the hunter's mind through the writings of philosophers and anthropologists and some contemporary hunters.

I realize now that it must be this fundamental truth that life depends on killing—this central fact of life that is side-stepped by my own cultural tradition—that has pulled me to the hunter. Without fully understanding why, I have been seeking insight into the mind and conscience of someone who faced this dilemma every day.

As I stand here in this place that has become part of the outer skin of my soul, I understand that the emotions that assault me now—sorrow, guilt, anticipation—are an original chemistry, just as timeless and universal as the bond between human and nature. Over the years, I have read the accounts of hunting rituals, preparations, and taboos, with the assumption that the careful actions were aimed at petition-ing success in the hunt. But now I wonder if another purpose wasn't just as important. The rituals must also have been a way to help the soul justify its part in the cycles of life and death.

For native cultures, the natural world is a powerful reality to which human lives are linked by spiritual and oral bonds. This is a view of the world that lies deep in our collective psyche and has become familiar to me over the years I have spent on this hillside. Now, it coalesces with new meaning as I recall my continuing search for the perfect tree, week after week, how it finally led me to this tree, once and then repeatedly, walk after walk. I remember that my feelings shifted; in place of feeling the randomness of fate, I had a feeling of rightness about this tree. I began to understand something that had never made sense to me before—how a hunter could feel that an animal offers him- or herself to be killed. With my intuition

159

that this tree was "right" came a feeling that the tree and I were both part of some larger pattern of life within which our small lives intersected.

And so I stand here, in front of this tree I have chosen. My reflections have left me feeling mostly at peace with my part in this event. But the moment is still harrowing.

What if I have made a mistake? What if, after all, I have misinterpreted the signs; what if I have killed in error?

While Nandi investigates something under a fallen madrone, its smooth red skin sparkling with frost, I hold this tree's small trunk firmly with my left hand. I place the saw at the base of the tree, close to the ground, so no stump will be left. As I pull the blade slowly through the tree's flesh, I am careful not to let its teeth wound the tree alongside, the one that I hope will benefit from less competition on this slope.

In the winter stillness, the rasp of the saw echoes down the length of the canyon. I wonder if other trees are listening, knowing. Despite my sense of rightness about this tree-cutting, the experience is not the clean and neat ritual I might hope for. The saw gets stuck, I feel clumsy, I grumble as I struggle to pull the blade. But in a few minutes, the violence is done. I lift the tree from its roots and hold it here, in my hand. The silence closes in again.

Nandi comes over to sniff what I have done. The small tree is still fresh with life; I can smell it, too. Breathing the juice of the fir into my lungs, I feel regret, gratitude—and something else. A hint of doubt. What if I have made a mistake? What if, after all, I have misinterpreted the signs; what if I have killed in error?

I understand in this flare of doubt that however much I may think I know about this land and its trees, about how trees grow and what they need to live, I will never know enough about the profound complexities of life on earth to be sure that I perform this act—that I kill—with moral certainty. The conviction of my human inadequacy expands within me.

And then, somehow, from somewhere, another emotion sweeps over me, and I am enveloped by a sweet and transforming humility, a feeling so unexpected that the experience can only be called a moment of grace. This feeling, which transcends the hunt and yet is utterly rooted in its essence, brings a sense of resolution to the impossible dilemmas with which I have been wrestling. I finally understand that humility is the key. Only through humility can the soul make peace with the terrible necessities of survival.

Getting to my feet, I carry the tree to the path, so I can take a good look. Yes, its branches are thick enough all the way around, as I had hoped. Before we turn toward home, I nod to the place from which I have taken the tree, give the tree a chance to bid farewell too. Then I hoist the trunk and needled limbs to my shoulders. While my head bobs among the sweet-smelling branches, Nandi dances ahead, and my boots crunch frost on the trail. Christmas feelings spread through the winter air.

> *And then, somehow, from somewhere, another emotion sweeps over me ...*

During the next ten days, as I go about the activities of Christmas—baking cookies, sweeping the floor, preparing a meal for friends—within the aura of the star-and animal-bedecked tree, I find myself contemplating the pattern of the hunt. In particular, I muse about the humility I felt—a feeling that I understand is part of a "right relation" to the largest powers of life, to God. Where, I wonder, did it come from?

I realize that the moment emerged from the convergence of many things: my wish for a Christmas tree, my attraction to this particular tree, my sense that the tree was a sentient being—and the inexplicable feeling that my life and the natural life of this place are linked, a sense of connection that has been quickening within me for twenty years.

Casting back, again, to what I know of hunting cultures, I understand that all the traditions of the hunt—prehunting rituals that attune a larger awareness, the code that admonishes killing only out of need, the respect given to the prey, the careful use of every part of the killed animals—derive from

this central sense of connection. The hunter knows that all life is bound together by power too subtle and complex to be fully understood. Humility, I think, must begin in this knowledge of sacred connection and be nourished by daily intimacy with the powerful, interrelated, living world.

And yet, for me, the act itself—this paradoxical, impossible act of taking a life—released the feeling. I contemplated again the moment, let myself sink again into the experience, with all its emotion and contradiction, trying to understand why. And I finally see that in this moment of the kill, the hunter stands at the intersection of the most profound of opposites—life and death. He knows not only that those opposites are linked—indeed that one becomes the other—but also that his life depends on being part of the transformation, part of the intimate, mysterious, ongoing communion of all life. I know that there are other ways to experience life's Oneness, but I wonder if this truth is ever so immediate, so palpable, so full of feeling as in the hunter's act.

35

WALTER MITTY HAS NOTHING ON ME

After all, he never introduced Liz Taylor to gloxinias.

By Bob Baker

▼   ▼   ▼

As I recall, it happened about a year after I started writing those "Plantlore" columns that they print in *Glox News*. You know, the newsletter of the Greater New York Chapter of the American Gloxinia and Gesneriad Society? Maybe some of you have seen them reprinted in *The Gloxinian*.

Well, anyway, here I am, sitting on the big stage at Carnegie Hall, staring out at the packed auditorium while the Program Chairman makes the introduction. I'm thinking of all the famous people who have been here before me—Tschaikovsky, Toscanini, Benny Goodman, even Ernest Hemingway—and trying to ignore the nervous tic in my left eyelid. I hear the chairman say that it gives him great pleasure to introduce me, the author of the Pulitzer Prize–winning "Plantlore" columns in *Glox News*, which columns, he notes, have brought about a tenfold increase in the plant society's membership in just one year. Thunderous applause erupts and rolls over me as I make my way to the rostrum.

I fidget with my notes until the applause finally dies down. After trying (but failing) to smile, I find my voice and begin.

"I would like to thank the chairman for his kind introduction," I remember myself saying. "Especially as I know that

163

his first choice as speaker for this evening was really ... Garrison Keillor."

Uncertain laughter breaks the silence of the great hall.

"Unfortunately, things have been looking up around Lake Wobegon ... ."

More confident laughter.

" ... and Garrison Keillor has fallen into a deep depression."

A satisfying explosion of guffaws.

"Still," I continue, "still, you shouldn't be too disappointed. What would a fellow of Scandinavian descent know about plants that grow in tropical rain forests?"

Murmurs of assent and nods of approval.

"For that you need someone named Baker."

A wave of laughter, then scattered applause.

"So I would just like you to know how very happy I am to be here, at Carnegie Hall, before 3,000 gesneriad enthusiasts, at the regular monthly meeting of the Greater New York Glox Society, where all the resolutions are strong, all the judges are good-looking, and all the seedlings are—"

I pause and scores of voices shout up at me across the footlights. "Above average!" they cry.

"Yes, above average," I say. "Thank you," I say. "Thank you very much."

Thunderous applause again rolls up and over me. Then I wake up.

I wonder if you, too, have such Walter Mitty-like dreams of glory. They come to me toward the end of every year as a kind of spontaneous holiday gift, a gift I would never dream of really giving myself—and one the real world is very unlikely to tender me.

It's early March. The telephone rings. The call is from the Gallery Chairman of the New York Flower Show. She informs me that my oft-entered *Episcia* 'Cleopatra' (you know that lovely confection, don't you?) has at long last won Best-in-Show. But that's not all, she tells me. She tells me she has two tickets for me to the Grand Gala Opening that evening. The TV news anchors, she says, are lining up to interview me.

"Two tickets?" I say. And the chairman says, "Yes, two tickets."

So I hang up and call Jackie O. and she says, yes, of course, she is free this evening, and, of course, she would be delighted to attend the Grand Gala Opening with me. It would just make her day.

I pause and scores of voices shout up at me across the footlights. "Thank you," I say. "Thank you very much." Thunderous applause again rolls up and over me.

A few hours later, me and Jackie, we stroll into the Flower Show just as if she did such things every day of her life. And when I introduce her around, she says she has never before met such interesting people. And could she join the Glox Society right away? And would I teach her how to grow sinningias? And I say, with a shy smile: Why not?

Oh—did I mention the time they decide not to have a Christmas tree at Rockefeller but to put up a tropical greenhouse in its place? And they want me to set it up—they've read my columns, you see—and then they want me to conduct tours for celebrity visitors who already have the key to the city. The mayor's a bit miffed, I hear, but that's life I tell him when he calls. When you grow African violets and gloxinias and write "Plantlore" columns, these things are bound to happen sooner or later.

And so, one evening, there I am showing the place to Elizabeth Taylor and Barbra Streisand who want especially to know what rhizomatous really means. And when I tell them, they still don't believe me until I insist that plant-lovers always tell the truth. Horticulturally speaking, you understand. How quaint, they say, and commence pulling on my arms, this way and that, to see if I'm breakable. Every man has his breaking point, they say. But I tell them they don't know plant-lovers who grow under lights—over egg crate—in leca stones—in wide

165

shallow pans. Yes, they agree, they don't. "But we'd sure like to," they say.

And just then I spot Burt Reynolds, his nose pressed up against a glass pane of the greenhouse like a kid at a candy store window, staring in at me and Elizabeth and Barbra ... and you know something? He's chlorophyll green with envy.

And now you know what I mean when I say that Walter Mitty has nothing on me.

The Greater New York Chapter of the American
Gloxinia and Gesneriad Society

36

FLOOD YIELDS

*The '93 Midwest Deluge gave gardeners
a surprising harvest.*

By Mary Swander

❖   ❖   ❖

Last spring, on Easter Monday, I knelt in my garden near Kalona, Iowa, to plant the season's first seeds: red-stemmed Swiss chard, deer tongue and Tom Thumb lettuce, radishes, tatsoi, and arugula. It was mid-April—already a couple weeks late for this sowing. But it was one of the first times the sun shone brightly enough to warm and dry up the soil, soil wet and soggy from almost nine months of continuous rain.

April is often a chaotic time of year for me, truly the cruelest month, with job pressures and sudden storms in my health or personal life often winding together and spiraling up the fence with enough force to make spring gardening not a pleasure, but a chore. Every seed that slipped from my fingers that Monday was coated with worries, regrets, and nagging thoughts: deadlines to be met, a row of unpaid doctor bills, a whole compost pile of lost loves. The meditational movements of planting did not quiet my racing mind. Instead, my emotions seemed way out ahead of my body. I wanted something to steady me, pull me back to the earth between my fingers.

Then suddenly, a horn honked and Moses appeared. Startled, I looked up and saw my 85-year-old Amish neighbor, the area "grosdaddie," leaning into my car, his arm through

167

the open window. His buggy was stationed in my yard, the reins of his horse looped around an old hitching post.

"Thought that'd rouse you out," Moses laughed. We hadn't seen each other since Thanksgiving, he having gone off to Florida with his wife for the winter.

I hurried out the gate.

He opened his arms and kissed me.

Both of us a bit stunned at this very non-Amish, non-midwestern display of emotion, we stood there a moment, silent, grinning, as the early morning light slanted down across Picayune Creek and over the former one-room schoolhouse I now call home.

After Moses's greeting and our reunion, I returned to my garden feeling renewed. Yes, I thought, things do need to be accomplished, yes, things do change. But that's all part of a bigger scheme. People come in and out of your life. Plants

Illustrations © Sandra Brooks Mathers

struggle out of the soil, grow, die, break down again. All living things have their cycles. That Easter Monday, my garden became for me a symbol not of stability, nor of change, but of stability within change.

Little did I know how I would have to cling to that notion the rest of the year.

Prairie plant roots grow deep and strong, holding in and filtering rainwater. Corn and soybean roots are not half as efficient.

The next four months were rain, raining, and rainy—intensifying and creating new fears each day. By the end of April, my Easter planting had all washed out, and my efforts to replant been thwarted by the dance of dark clouds and mighty mud puddles. The corn was only shin high by the Fourth of July when gigantic lightning bolts crackled the sky and the Picayune rose so fast that it sent my neighbor's hogs swimming for higher ground. Two weeks later, storms hammered us again and the sows' newly delivered litters washed away downstream.

With the soil compacted, the weather consistently cool, and the sun shining a total of only 19 days all summer, every gardener in the region felt the effects of the Great Flood of 1993. Some noticed only a delay in maturation, their broccoli and cabbage late to head. Others lost their tomato crops, blights and fungi riddling the plump fruit. Those closer to major rivers and lakes saw their whole gardens go under for weeks at a time, the tips of their bean poles poking up out of the water. Gardeners in Des Moines watched in horror as a man just off Interstate-80 bulldozed his whole magnificent plot of young vegetables, scooping the dirt up into the air and dropping it down again in piles to build a dike around his house.

While news crews filmed houses cracking in two, floating down the Mississippi River, and interviewed flood victims living by the side of the road, not much thought was given to garden loss. But once the waters receded, clean-up efforts told a tale of at least double and perhaps triple horticultural destruction: We lost much of this year's crop, along with a portion of last year's in storage—and next year's planting is in question.

I drove past Hannibal, Missouri, on one of the first days the river road was open in early August, the water parting on each side of the pavement like the Red Sea, and found a tangle of debris—cornstalks and bean plants from farm and garden—washed up on the shoulder. In Chelsea, Iowa, a small town on the Iowa River that was evacuated five times this year, a team of teenage Mennonites cleaned out water-logged basements at the end of July, dumping wheelbarrow after wheelbarrow of canned vegetables on the trash pile. And now, with the ground so saturated that the Corps of Engineers is urging us to leave up our sandbags throughout the winter, we're wondering if flood waters will return and prevent us from even turning over the soil next spring.

"From now on, I'm going to garden differently," Carl, a friend in Iowa City, told me. "I'm choosing only the most hardy, resilient varieties for my plot."

A friend near the Saylorville Reservoir in Ankeny, Iowa, where the lake waters twice covered his garden this summer and came within 100 yards of his house, found himself becoming more resilient. "When I was flooded two years ago, I thought the world was coming to an end. I dug all sorts of ditches, replanted everything, and looked upon the whole event as a huge, man-versus-nature challenge. This time, I've learned to accept and go with it."

Once I thought of my garden and the whole flood as a lesson in resilience and renewal, I began to see a majesty in the bigger event.

As I struggled to bring in my own late harvest, the okra reaching its normal height just as frost threatened to kill its pink blossoms, I realized this summer has brought lessons of resilience to us all. Carl told me that when he dug his garlic this summer, he was delighted with the big, healthy-looking bulbs. But when he cut into one, he discovered they were skin- and meat-less—nothing but papery pulp. We flood gardeners appear to be the opposite. We may look the worse for wear, but this year's conditions have toughened us, outside and in. Cut us open and we can still stand up to the most intense stress.

Midwestern spiritual leaders from the far right to the New Age left called the flood a "cleansing," a time to wash out the old and welcome the new. Some conservative religious groups thought the flood a punishment for our sins. My Easter Monday garden interactions opened the gate to a different perspective, one of personal calm. Pressures and losses seemed less crises and more parts of a natural whole.

But as the rains kept up, washing the soil down-stream, the straight-ened rivers cutting faster and deeper at their banks, the fields around me turning into lakes, my vision enlarged. The flood forced me  to stop and view the scene with a wider lens. I still had a hard time buying the punitive-God approach, but did find a bit of truth in the biblical adage that the sins of the father would be paid for by the sons. The almost complete destruction of the prairie contributed to the severity of the flooding in Iowa. Prairie plant roots grow deep and strong, holding in and filtering rainwater. Corn and soybean roots are not half as efficient.

As basic and satisfying as it is, gardening, too, in its small way displaced prairie. Gardening is, after all, an unnatural, ethnocentric act. Our ancestors, who pioneered this land of promise, of milk and honey, wanted to eat the foods they were accustomed to in Europe.

If our great-grandparents had foraged for more native species, as the Native Americans had for centuries before them, they would have preserved the integrity of the prairie. Of course, population and time pressures make this difficult on today's large scale, but we should at least take stock of the reality now and concede that, as hard as we try, we will never "tame" the land. If we alter one part of the ecosystem, we will eventually have to cope with the imbalance that act causes in another. The destruction of the prairie did not bring the summer's deluge, but it did exacerbate its effects. This year, as never before, we were forced to face the power of nature, its enormous ability to have its way—and both our significance and insignificance in that event.

This summer I, too, learned "my place," in my garden and in the larger environment. Once I let go of my own worries, once I thought of my garden and the whole flood as a lesson in resilience and renewal, I began to see a majesty in the bigger event. While half my potato crop rotted in the ground, cattails—tall, spiky, and strong— shot up in my ditch. While my beets reached only half their normal size, huge, great blue herons circled overhead.

One night, late in the summer, Moses dropped by to eye the Picayune, assessing how far it had risen out of its banks.

"It's really been something this year, hasn't it?" I asked.

"It's been something, all right," Moses replied.

We fell silent, Moses and I, standing together again near my garden on the hill, watching as the summer of '93, and some of our promised land, flowed past in the valley below.

37

THE FALL OF WINTER

I don't like winter. I don't. I don't. I don't.

By Eric Grissell

❄   ❄   ❄

Anyone who gardens knows there are only three seasons: spring when the weather is fickle, summer when it isn't, and winter when the weather is even more fickle. Most nongardeners think there is another season called fall. They are quite wrong. Fall is a concept created by a New England Chamber of Commerce as tourist propaganda. Gardeners know that fall is a verb, not a noun, and describes what happens in the first week of winter. As in, "All the leaves fall down."

All summer long I've been busy gardening, with nary a second to sit and think about what I'm doing when all of a sudden ... BANG, it's over. One day, it's daylight saving time, the next it's winter. Yesterday the crickets cricketed and today they are buried under 16 feet of snow. Summer has ended, winter's begun, and all that's left for me to do is to sit and mold.

Sorry, I am not a winter gardener. I don't like winter. I've said so before and I'll say so again ... to anyone who listens. Winter is cold. I don't like cold. My joints don't like cold. My muscles (such as they are) don't like cold. My brain doesn't like cold. In winter people take me for dull-witted because I can't get two thoughts connected one in front of the other.

(This problem afflicts me other times of the year as well, but I think that is another story entirely.) Someone asks a question about pansies or when should they plant next year's seeds and then awaits an answer. They wait quite a while, actually, for I have none. My brain goes dormant for the winter just like a seed, and I cannot converse in the normal language of gardening again until the spring thaws. My guess is there isn't enough antifreeze in my blood and the hoses to my brain freeze. During winter, even if I could converse in "gardening," most people are speaking some other language unknown to me. It is a strange, alien language called "football." Fortunately, I am not multilingual.

Yesterday the crickets cricketed and today they are buried under 16 feet of snow.

So far as I can determine, cold serves only one purpose and that is to remind you of how good warm really is when you have it. This derives from the school of philosophical thought (or lack thereof) that rationalizes bad things by telling you that bad is good because it illustrates just how good "good" really is going to get if you wait long enough. Frankly, most of us don't have that kind of time. Simple examples of this theory are that dieting teaches us to appreciate food; life on earth teaches us to appreciate what is to come; and working in our own garden teaches us to appreciate anyone else's.

One of the basic tenets of this school is that the only reason to garden is because it feels so good when you stop. So they stop as often as possible. This philosophy is followed mostly by the order of the Weekenders for Energetic Entropy and Devastated Suburbs (WEEDS)—a group of housepayers dedicated to the proposition that today's house is best set off by the surrealism of stark barrenness. Their motto: "I'd rather do anything else than take care of the yard." Endless hours are spent washing the paint off the car, watching flies land on one's stomach, analyzing the liquid level in a beer can, or resting from the exhaustion of doing all three over a two-day weekend. Occasionally a lawn gets cut—but only some one else's!

Basically, I don't want to stop gardening, even in winter, because I'm afraid that one spring the old machinery isn't going to start up again. Not only do the hoses to the brain freeze, but the assorted pulleys, wheels, cables, crankshafts, and valves rust if they don't get used. My feeling is that it's better to keep at full steam all year than to need a jump start in the spring.

So please pardon me while I hunt up my long-johns, woolens, parka, muffler, balaklava, crampons, and ice-axe, and head out for the garden. I think I just heard some leaves fall.

38

SANGUINARIA

If we didn't talk about it, maybe it wouldn't be real.

By A. Jenkins Farmer III

❁   ❁   ❁

I can't remember his name. I've tried. The last time I remember seeing his name was the day he died. There was a pink phone memo in my message box. His name was on it. The pink phone memo said that he had died that morning.

He was the volunteer who came to the Botanical Garden on Tuesdays to help in the wildflower display.

I knew he was sick. When we ate lunch in the cafeteria, he'd only order a vanilla milkshake. Sometimes he'd sit all hunched over on the edge of the boardwalk that ran through the wildflower garden. He said he'd be OK.

I knew he was lonely, too. He always asked what I did after work, what gardens I visited, what my friends were like. He hadn't lived in the South for very long. I knew he wanted to join in, to go to a movie. I would have liked to have had him along.

But I was too busy. I had two jobs and my plans were always set. I didn't want to complicate my life any further.

We were friends at work. We dug more holes for three-inch Solomon Seal plants than I care to remember. We learned that Solomon Seal is a healing herb; used to soothe poison ivy and internal pains. We wore rain suits in the heat of August to protect ourselves while we pulled poison ivy out of the woods. He was the only person who would help with that. We had fun and always got a lot of work done. We talked about centipede grass a lot. He said it hurt his feet. He was from the North where, he said, grass is soft. He missed soft grass.

He missed his friends and family, especially his brother. He missed seeing the leaves change that year. Leaves, like a lot of things, don't seem to change in the South.

I got the first pink phone memo, the one that said he was in the hospital, late one afternoon. I was going to call the next day, but I had a buying trip. I had a great time walking around the nursery in the rain. Trying to pick out good pots of senesing bloodroot, river oats, and green and gold. He would have loved that day. He would have loved walking around a muddy nursery and the pots and the rain and the plants and the trucks.

It was a long, busy day. When I got back to the office at the Garden, I was still wet, still had potting soil glued to my hands. I tried to pick up my mail without getting it dirty. There was a second pink phone memo on the top of my mail. The one that said he had died that morning. The one with his name on it.

I called his house, but a machine answered. I called his job. They said he had died of food poisoning. I sort of believed it so that I could enjoy the Thanksgiving weekend with my relatives.

I wondered about his family. Did they get a call from a stranger, a nurse or a doctor, saying that their 35-year-old son just died of food poisoning? Did they believe it?

I sort of halfway believed it, until Monday morning when I set out to pull the poison ivy from the bed where the bloodroot was supposed to go. I knew I would be doing this alone from now on. I was sad and I was angry. I knew he hadn't died of food poisoning. I'd known it long before I heard the whispering around work, about what he'd die of.

I'm still angry. Afraid, too. Angry with and afraid of myself and him and everyone who says that we shouldn't talk about that kind of stuff.

I could have been his friend. A real friend. I could have asked about his health, his home, his brother. I didn't want to know. It was all easier left unsaid. I talked about everything else. I never asked the glaring question. I didn't want to see the truth—any more than he did.

He could have been my friend, too. He could have said, "Listen, we are going to talk about this because it's a real problem. You need to know and I need to talk."

Now I think I would have thanked him for his honesty. But maybe he knew better. Maybe he knew all the reasons why people like him don't talk about it. That people who talk might lose jobs, friends, family, freedom. Before they lose the rest.

Not long afterwards, I moved north, to a city. People talk about it a little more freely here. But just a little.

I planted the bloodroot before I left. I heard that the flowers were beautiful the next March. Bloodroot flowers are simple and pure white. They only last a day or two.

I didn't see them.

39

PARADISE COMES SLOWLY

*Some plants—and people—take
a long time to flower.*

By Jeff Lowenfels

❖   ❖   ❖

About ten years ago, I was sitting at my desk with a Park's spring garden catalog on my lap. I spied a picture of a *Strelitzia reginae,* aka Bird of Paradise, my daughter's favorite flowering plant as a result of a trip to Hawaii. Its blooms look like the head of an exotic parrot, mimicking feathers of red, orange, blue, purple, and yellow.

Underneath the picture of this flowering wonder was an enticing caption that read: "Bird of Paradise, Strelitzia. Exciting, distinct, long-lasting flowers; superb for arrangements. Four-foot plants with huge leaves, big exotic flowers on long stems."

As if that weren't enough, the pitch continued: "Grow indoors in winter … ." I knew what I had to do. I had a three-year-old daughter who loved Bird of Paradise flowers, and I was determined to grow her some. So what if we lived in Alaska. *She* had faith in me. How could I fail?

So, ten years ago, I sent off $1.75 and got back five pea-size seeds. With visions of the blooming plant as seen in the catalog (and of Mickey Mouse climbing the beanstalk in the fabled cartoon), and buoyed by the words "Grow indoors in winter," I immediately planted them.

We waited and waited, and then one day, as much to my amazement as anybody else's, one of the seeds actually germinated. The months it had taken required much patience. I was lulled into thinking that flowers couldn't be too far away. As the catalog predicted, I did soon have a plant with huge leaves. In fact, after ten years, ours has a dozen leaves, each shaped like a canoe paddle with a blade one and a half feet long and five or six inches wide. One or two new leaves are added every year, and each time, until they unfold, I eagerly anticipate a flower bud.

Over the past ten years, I've repotted the plant a number of times. At first the roots were as thin as hairs, and I used a two-inch pot. Now the plant's main roots look like a one-inch gardening hose, and they strain the plant's three-foot plastic pot. I don't think I can find a bigger pot. I wouldn't have any place to keep it even if I could. Still no blooms.

Every summer I've taken the plant out to some protected location and let it be. Lately it has had a favored spot on the southeast side of the garage, from where, each fall, I try to lug it back indoors with the least possible amount of effort. A *Strelitzia* in a three-foot pot is a weighty matter. As I risk my back, I mutter the famous "Grow indoors in winter" over and over.

Sometime around the fourth or fifth flowerless year, I did some research on the cultivation of Bird of Paradise plants. My daughter was asking questions. Maybe I was doing something wrong. I learned, instead, that most of these plants are propagated by rhizome division. Seed-grown plants will flower, but take many years. Somewhere I read that one shouldn't even expect Bird of Paradise flowers until the plant's seventh year. I never saw those words in Park's description of *Strelitzia*. Maybe that is what they meant by "exotic."

I also learned that the plant did best if given 55-degree nights and five to ten degrees warmer conditions during the day. These happen to be the conditions Alaskans can most easily provide when they "Grow indoors in winter." I was determined to wait it out.

So year in and year out, I've cared for this seed-grown *Strelitzia*. It has been in the living room, it has rested in a warm, sunny bathroom, and has recuperated in the greenhouse. It has had sunny, southern bedroom exposure and dry living-room life. Until now, however, it has simply refused to bloom.

When I first started growing the plant, I was pretty proud of it. I would point it out to friends: "Hey, look what's growing here." Even my dad was fairly impressed. After a while, however, people began to ask how old the plant was and if it had ever flowered. "Gee, it's that old and has never flowered? Why do you keep it?" I resisted the urge to chuck it. I could get this thing to bloom. I had to. I had promised my daughter.

Finally, after ten years, the *Strelitzia* has put up a flower stalk. There is no longer any doubt. It is going to flower. Of course, my daughter is a lot wiser now. She is too old to believe in Dad the way a three-year-old does. Besides, she grows her own miracles in the greenhouse and gardens outdoors right alongside me. At thirteen, she no longer needs me to try and impress her.

For my part, I am not sure I am that much wiser after these ten years, though I do have a pretty good idea of how to bring up a daughter. It takes all the care and, above all, the same kind of patience, humor, and dedication you need to get a seed-grown *Strelitzia* to flower.

Illustration © Jean Jenkins

40

WEEDS ARE US

We are the problem—and the solution.

By Michael Pollan

O   O   O

Ralph Waldo Emerson, who as a lifelong gardener really should have known better, once said that a weed is simply a plant whose virtues we haven't yet discovered. "Weed" is not a category of nature but a human construct, a defect of our perception. This kind of attitude, which comes out of an old American strain of romantic thinking about wild nature, can get you into trouble. At least it did me. For I had Emerson's pretty conceit in mind when I planted my first flower bed, and the result was not a pretty thing.

Having read perhaps too much Emerson, and too many of the sort of gardening book that advocates "wild gardens" and nails a pair of knowing quotation marks around the word weed (a sure sign of ecological sophistication), I sought to make a flower bed that was as "natural" as possible. Rejecting all geometry (too artificial!), I cut a more or less kidney-shaped bed in the lawn, pulled out the sod, and divided the bare ground into irregular patches that I roughly outlined with a bit of ground limestone. Then I took packets

Illustrations © Sandra Brooks Mathers

182

of annual seeds—bachelor's buttons, nasturtiums, nicotianas, cosmos, poppies (California and Shirley both), cleomes, zinnias, and sunflowers—and broadcast a handful of each into the irregular patches, letting the seeds fall wherever nature dictated. No rows: this bed's arrangement would be natural. I waited eagerly for the seeds to sprout.

Pigweed sprouted first, though at the time I was so ignorant that I figured this vigorous upstart must be zinnia, or sunflower. I had had no prior acquaintance with pigweed (it grew nowhere else on the property), and did not deduce that it was a weed until I noticed it was coming up in every single one of my irregular patches. Within a week the entire bed was clothed in tough, hairy pigweeds, and it was clear that I would have to start pulling them out if I ever expected to see my intended annuals. The absence of rows or paths made weeding difficult, but I managed to at least thin the lusty pigweeds, and the annuals, grateful for the intervention on their behalf, finally pushed themselves up out of the earth. Finding the coast relatively clear, they started to grow in earnest.

I liked how wild my garden was. Call me Ecology Boy.

That first summer, my little annual meadow thrived, pretty much confirming to the picture I'd had in mind when I planted it. Sky-blue drifts of bachelor's buttons flowed seamlessly into hot spots thick with hunter-orange and fire-engine poppies, behind which rose great sunflower towers. The nasturtiums poured their sand-dollar leaves into neat, low mounds dabbed with crimson and lemon, and the cleomes worked out their intricate architectures high in the air. Weeding this dense tangle was soon all but impossible, but after the pigweed scare I'd adopted a more or less laissez-faire policy toward the uninvited. The weeds that moved in were ones I was willing to try to live with: jewelweed (a gangly orange-flowered relative of impatiens), foxtail grass, clover, shepherd's purse, inconspicuous Galinsoga, and Queen Anne's lace, the sort of weed Emerson must have had in mind, with its ivory lace flowers (as pretty as anything you might plant) and edible, carrotlike root. That first year a pretty vine also crept in, a refuge from the surrounding lawn. It twined its way up the sunflower stalks and in August unfurled white, trumpet-shaped flowers that resembled morning glory.

What right had I to oust this delicate vine? To decide that the flowers I planted were more beautiful than ones the wind had sown? I liked how wild my garden was, how peaceably my cultivars seemed to get along with their wild relatives. And I liked how unneurotic I was being about "weeds." Call me Ecology Boy.

My romance of the weed did not survive a second summer. The annuals, which I had allowed to set seed the previous year, did come back, but they proved a poor match for the weeds, who returned heavily reinforced. It was as though news of this sweet deal (this chump gardener!) had spread through the neighborhood over the winter, for the weed population burgeoned, both in number and in kind. Recognizing that what I now tended was a weed garden, and having been taught that a gardener should know the name of every plant in his care, I consulted a few field guides and drew up an inventory of my collection. In addition to the species I've already mentioned, I had milkweed, pokeweed, smartweed, St.-John's-wort, quack grass, crabgrass, plantain, dandelion, bladder campion, flea-bane, butter-and-eggs, timothy, mallow, birds-foot trefoil, lamb's quarters, chickweed, purslane, curly dock, goldenrod, sheep sorrel, burdock, Canada thistle, and stinging nettle. I'm sure I've missed another dozen, and misidentified a few, but this will give you an idea of the various fruits of my romanticism. What had begun as a kind of idealized wildflower meadow now looked like a roadside tangle, and if I let it go another year, would probably pass for a vacant lot.

Since this had not been my aesthetic aim, I set about reclaiming my garden—or at least to arrest the process at "country road-side" before it degenerated to "abandoned railroad siding." I would be enlightened about it, though, pardoning the weeds I liked and expelling all the rest. I was pre-pared to tolerate the fleabane, holding aloft their sunny clouds of tiny asterlike flowers, or milkweed, with its interesting seedpods, but bully weeds like burdock, Canada thistle, and stinging nettle had to go. Unfortunately, the weeds I liked least proved to be the best armed and most recalcitrant. Burdock, whose giant clubfoot leaves shade out ev-ery other plant for yards around, holds the earth in a death grip. Straining to pull out its mile-long taproot, you feel like a boy try-ing to arm-wrestle a man. Inevitably the root breaks before it yields, with the result that, in a few days' time, you have two tough burdocks where before there had been one. All I seemed able to do was help my bur-dock reproduce. I felt less like an extermi-nator of these weeds than their midwife.

That pretty vine with the morning glory blossoms turned out to be another hydra-headed monster. Bindweed, as it's called, grows like kudzu and soon threatened to blanket the entire garden. It can grow only a foot or so high without support, so it casts about like a blind man, lurching this way then that, until it finds a suitable plant to lean on 185 and eventually smother. Here too my efforts at eradication proved counterproductive.

Bindweed, whose roots may reach ten feet down, can reproduce either by seed or human-aided cloning. For its root is as brittle as a fresh snapbean; put a hoe to it and it breaks into a dozen pieces, each of which will sprout an entire new plant. It is as though the bindweed's evolution took the hoe into account. By attacking it at its root—the approved strategy for eradicating most weeds—I played right into the insidious bindweed's strategy for world domination.

Now what would Emerson have to say? I had given all my weeds the benefit of the doubt, acknowledged their virtues and allotted them a place. I had treated them, in other words, as garden plants. But they did not behave as garden plants. They differed from my cultivated varieties not merely by a factor of human esteem. No, they seemed truly a different order of being, more versatile, better equipped, swifter, craftier—simply more adroit at the work of being a plant. What garden plant can germinate in 36 minutes, as a tumbleweed can? What cultivar can produce 400,000 seeds on a single flower stalk, as the mullein does? Or hitch its seeds to any passing animal, like the burdock? Or travel a foot each day, as kudzu can?

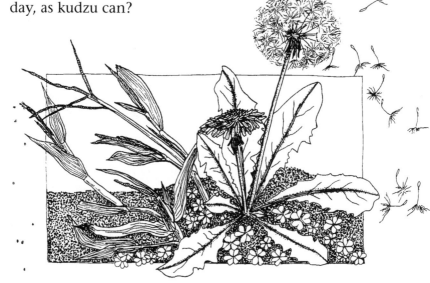

My own experience in the garden has convinced me that weeds represent a different order of being. I found support for this hunch in the field guides and botany books I consulted when I was trying to identify my weeds. As I searched these volumes for the *Noms de bloom* of my marauders, I jotted down each species' preferred habitat. Here are a few of the most typical: "waste places and roadside"; "open sites"; "old fields, waste places"; "cultivated and waste ground"; "old fields, roadsides, lawns, gardens"; "lawns, gardens, disturbed sites."

What this list suggests is that weeds are not superplants: they don't grow everywhere, which explains why, for all their vigor, they haven't covered the globe entirely. Weeds, as the field guides indicate, are plants particularly well adapted to man-made places. They don't grow in forests or prairies—in "the wild." Weeds thrive in gardens, meadows, lawns, vacant lots, railroad sidings, hard by dumpsters and in the cracks of sidewalks. They grow where we live, in other words, and hardly anywhere else.

Weeds, contrary to what the romantics assumed, are not wild. They are as much a product of cultivation as the hybrid tea rose. They do better than garden plants for the simple reason that they are better adapted to life in a garden. For where garden plants have been bred for a variety of traits (tastiness, nutritiousness, size, aesthetic appeal), weeds have evolved with just one end in view: the ability to thrive in ground that man has disturbed. At this they are very accomplished indeed.

Weeds stand at the forefront of evolution; no doubt they are evolving in my garden at this very moment, their billions of offspring self-selecting for new tactics to outwit my efforts and capitalize on any opening in my garden. Weeds are nature's ambulance chasers, carpetbaggers, and confidence men. 187

Virtually every crop in general cultivation has its weed imposter, a kind of botanical doppelganger that has evolved to mimic the appearance as well as the growth rate of the cultivated crop and so ensure its survival. Some of these imposters, such as wild oats, are so versatile that they can alter their appearance depending on the crop they are imitating, like an insidious agricultural Fifth Column. According to Sara B. Stein's botany, *My Weeds*, wild oats growing in a field of alternating rows of spring and winter barley will mimic the habits of either crop, *depending on the row*. Stein, whose book is a trove of information about weeds, also tells of a rice mimic that became so troublesome that researchers planted a purple variety of rice to expose the weeds once and for all. Within a few years, the weed-rice had turned purple too.

St.-John's-wort, daisies, dandelions, crabgrass, timothy, clover, pigweed, lamb's-quarters, buttercup, mullein, Queen Anne's lace, plantain, yarrow—not one of these species grew here before the Puritans landed.

And yet as resourceful and aggressive as weeds may be, they cannot survive without us any more than a garden plant can. Without man to create crop land and lawns and vacant lots, most weeds would soon vanish. Bindweed, which seems so formidable in the field and garden, can grow nowhere else. It lives by the plow as much as we do.

To learn all this was somehow liberating. My weeds were no more natural than my garden plants, had no greater claim to the space they were vying for. Those smug quotes in which naturalists like to coddle weeds were merely a conceit. My battles with weeds did not bespeak alienation from nature, or some irresponsible drive to dominate it. Had Emerson's own disciple, Henry David Thoreau, known this when he planted his bean field at Walden, perhaps he would not have troubled himself so about "what right had I to oust St. Johnswort, and the rest, and to break up their ancient herb garden?"

Thoreau considered his wormwood, pigweed, sorrel, and St.-John's-wort part of nature, his beans part of civilization.

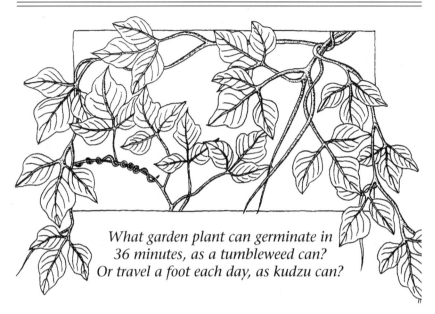

*What garden plant can germinate in
36 minutes, as a tumbleweed can?
Or travel a foot each day, as kudzu can?*

He looked to the American landscape, as many of us do, for a path that would lead him out of history and into nature, and this led him to value what grew "naturally" over that which man planted. But as it turns out history is inescapable, even at Walden. Much of the flora in the Walden landscape is as historical as his beans, his books, even the Mexican battlefield he makes his bean field a foil for. Had Thoreau brought a field guide with him to Walden, he might have noted that most of the weeds that came up in his garden were alien species, brought to America by the colonists. St.-John's-wort, far from being an ancient Walden resident, was brought to America in 1696 by a band of fanatical Rosicrucians who claimed the herb had the power to exorcise evil spirits. You want to privilege this over beans?

It's hard to imagine the American landscape without St.-John's-wort, daisies, dandelions, crabgrass, timothy, clover, pigweed, lamb's-quarters, buttercup, mullein, Queen Anne's lace, plantain, or yarrow, but not one of these species grew here before the Puritans landed. America in fact had few indigenous weeds, for the simple reason that it had little disturbed 189 ground. The Indians lived so lightly on the land that they created few habitats for weeds to take hold in. No plow, no bindweed. But by as early as 1663, when John Josselyn compiled a list "of such plantes as have sprung up since the English planted and kept cattle in New England," he found, among others, couch grass, dandelion, sow thistle, shepherd's purse, groundsel, dock, mullein, plantain, and chickweed.

Some of these weeds were brought over deliberately: the colonists prized dandelion as a salad green, and used plantain (which is millet) to make bread. Other weed seeds, though, came by accident—in forage, in the earth used for shipboard ballast, even in pants cuffs and cracked boot soles. Once here, the weeds spread like wildfire. According to Alfred W. Crosby, the ecological historian, the Indians considered the Englishman a botanical Midas, able to change the flora with his touch; they called plantain "Englishman's foot" because it seemed to spring up wherever the white man stepped. (Hiawatha claimed that the spread of the plant presaged the doom of the wilderness.) Though most weeds traveled with white men, some, like the dandelion, raced west of their own accord (or possibly with the help of the Indians, who quickly discovered the plant's virtues), arriving well ahead of the pioneers. Thus the supposedly virgin landscape upon which the westward settlers gazed had already been marked by civilization. However, those same pioneers did not gaze out on tumbleweed, that familiar emblem of the untamed western landscape. Tumbleweed did not arrive in America until the 1870s, when a group of Russian immigrants settled in Bonhomme County, South Dakota, intending to grow flax. Mixed in with their flax seeds were a few seeds of a weed well known on the steppes of the Ukraine: tumbleweed.

European weeds thrived here, in a matter of years changing the face of the American landscape, helping to create what

To weed is to bring culture to nature. It is not a nuisance of gardening, but its very essence.

we now take to be our country's abiding "nature." Why should these species have prospered so? Probably because the Europeans who brought them got busy making the land safe for weeds by razing the forests, plowing fields, burning prairies, and keeping grazing animals. And just as the Europeans helped smooth the way for their weeds, weeds helped smooth the way for Europeans.

Working in concert, European weeds and European humans proved formidable ecological imperialists, rapidly driving out native species and altering the land to suit themselves. The new plant species thrived because they were consummate cosmopolitans, opportunists superbly adapted to travel and change. In a sense, the invading species had less in common with the retiring, provincial plants they ousted than with the Europeans themselves. Or perhaps that should be put the other way around. "If we confine the concept of weeds to species adapted to human disturbance," writes Jack R. Harland in *Crops and Man,* "then man is by definition the first and primary weed under whose influence all other weeds have evolved."

Weeds are not the Other. Weeds are us.

There's no going back. Even Yellowstone, our country's greatest "wilderness," stands in need of careful management— it's too late to simply "leave it alone." I have no idea, for example, what the best fire policy for Yellowstone might be, but I do know that men and women, armed with scientific knowledge and acting through human institutions, will have to choose and then implement one. In doing so, they will have to grapple with the fact that, long before Yellowstone was declared a "wilderness area," Indians were setting fires in it; were these "natural"? If the goal is to restore Yellowstone to its pre-Columbian condition, their policy may well have to include the setting of fires. They will also have to decide how many tourists Yellowstone can support, whether wolves should be reintroduced to keep the elk population from exploding, and a host of other complicated questions. Today, even Yellowstone must be "gardened."

191

A century after Thoreau wrote that "in wildness is the preservation of the world," Wendell Berry, the Kentucky poet and farmer, added a corollary that would have made no sense at all to Thoreau, and yet that is necessary. Berry wrote that "in human culture is the preservation of wildness." I take him to mean that it's too late now to do nothing. Only human wisdom and forbearance can save places like Yellowstone.

Thoreau, and his many heirs among contemporary naturalists and radical environmentalists, assume that human culture is the problem, not the solution. So they urge us to shed our anthropocentrism and learn to live among other species as equals. This sounds like a fine, ecological idea, until you realize that the earth would be even worse off if we started behaving any more like animals than we already do. The survival strategy of most species is to extend their dominion as far and as brutally as they can, until they run up against some equally brutal natural limit that checks their progress. Isn't this exactly what we've been doing?

What sets us apart from other species is culture, and what is culture but forbearance? Conscience, ethical choice, memory, discrimination: it is these very human and decidedly unecological faculties that offer the planet its last best hope. It is true that, historically, we've concentrated on exercising these faculties in the human rather than the natural estate, but that doesn't mean they cannot be exercised there. Indeed, this is the work that now needs to be done: to bring more culture to our conduct in nature, not less.

If I seem to have wandered far afield of weeds, consider what weeding is: the process by which we make informed choices in nature, discriminate between good and bad, apply our intelligence and sweat to the earth. To weed is to bring culture to nature—which is why we say, when we are weeding, that we are cultivating the soil. Weeding, in this sense, is not a nuisance that follows from gardening, but its very essence. And, like gardening, weeding at a certain point becomes an obligation. As I learned in my flower bed, mere neglect won't bring back "nature."

In this, my yard is not so different from the rest of the world. We cannot live in it without changing nature irrevocably; having done so, we're obliged to tend to the consequences of the changes we've wrought, which is to say, to weed. "Weeding" is what will save places like Yellowstone, but only if we recognize the need to cultivate our own nature, too. For though we may be the earth's gardeners, we are also its weeds. And we won't get anywhere until we come to terms with this crucial ambiguity about our role—that we are at once the problem and the only possible solution to the problem.